Touchst

An Activity Book for Adult Leaders

Robert L. Miller
Gerard P. Weber

TABOR
PUBLISHING

Valencia, California   Allen, Texas

Send all inquiries to:
Tabor Publishing
25115 Avenue Stanford, Suite 130
Valencia, California 91355

Printed in the United States of America

ISBN 0-89505-450-7

1 2 3 4 5   91 90 89 88 87

Contents

CONTENTS

Acknowledgments

We are grateful to the many people and the many books that have suggested the activities included in this book. Because the activities have been changed and adapted to meet the needs of particular groups, it is no longer possible to pinpoint the source of each one. We hope that in the same way, the users of this book will shorten, combine, and rearrange the activities to meet the specific requirements of their own groups.

Introduction

This book springs from our experience and our firm conviction that getting in touch with oneself is the basis of a fulfilling life as well as the foundation for Christian community. It is a collection of activities that can be used as touchstones to help people make contact with their true feelings as well as their ideas about themselves, God, Jesus, and the Church. Over the years, we have used these activities to help people get in touch with their stories and clarify the meaning of their lives. We have found these activities to be powerful instruments for getting people involved in various church groups and organizations, for building relationships within a group, and for fostering self-awareness by helping people see the relationship of Scripture to their lives. The activities also help people see that the spiritual life is a journey with many crises and turning points.

FOSTERING COMMUNITY

Christian community is a dynamic network of relationships. But before people can enter fully into dialog with others and, through this dialog, grow in relationships, they must understand and grapple with their roots. Community results when individuals clarify and organize their life stories and share them with others. Every gathering of a group of people, be it large or small, can become an opportunity to share faith and to experience growth in community. All individuals and subgroups in the larger community, as well as the entire community itself, have their own stories to tell about their relationships with themselves, with the Lord, and with the larger world in which they exist. It is in sharing these experiences with others in small groups that people grow and take part in spiritual discovery.

STORYTELLING—THE BASIS OF FAITH

Our own stories—that is, our own life experiences—are where we discover God's living presence. Just as the Israelites could look back on their long, difficult journey through the desert and see God's hand in the midst of their struggles, so we need to look back at our own journey to discover the reality of God in our lives. Amid the trials in the desert, it was not clear to the Hebrews that they were loved by God, that God was present to meet their needs, that they were really God's people in a special way, or that they were a community at all. It was only in reflecting on their experiences and getting in touch with their history that they could recognize the hand of God in their lives and realize that they were indeed a people with a special identity, that they were the people of God, and that God had been with them every step of the way.

The telling of life stories is the oldest and perhaps the most effective way for individuals and for groups of people to understand where they come from, where they are, and where they are going. It helps them make sense out of their experiences and express their identity both as individuals and as a community.

Storytelling involves more than the mere recitation of facts. It must also involve one's feelings, one's interpretation of the meaning of events, and the way in which one sees the events related to other events—past, present, and future. It puts one in touch with his or her basic attitude toward reality.

Each person has a unique story to tell because people are the sum of their experiences and of the way they have interpreted and understood those experiences. We all have had different positive and negative influences in our lives, different experiences, and different relationships with others and with God. Storytelling helps us acknowledge, accept, and take ownership of these life stories. In doing so, we are better able to plan how we wish to live. Sharing these stories helps us understand one another better and so develop a common bond, a sense of unity, and a sense of community with the people who share our view of life.

STORYTELLING AND SCRIPTURE

Most of the activities in this book have to do with Scripture because such activities help us realize that the people mentioned in Scripture experienced exactly the same feelings that we have and that the Hebrews and early Christians had to go through the same processes that we go through today. When we see our lives in light of the Scripture stories, we also see that other options are open to us. We realize that other people have faced similar situations but have marched to a different tune—a tune set to the melody of faith.

ASSUMPTIONS

This book recognizes the fact that human beings develop through stages. Adults do not learn in the same way as children. This book reflects nine basic assumptions to keep in mind when working with adults.

1. Human life is the focal point of God's activity in the world. Scripture records the activity of God's self-revelation in the lives of people. By reflecting on our lives and experiences, we can learn a great deal about how we are to grow. But by reflecting on the life of Jesus and the other great people in Scripture, we learn how to grow as Christians. Jesus, Moses, Abraham, Peter—even Judas—all had human experiences similar to ours. When we look at their lives, identifying the processes at work and seeing that they are the same as those at work in our own lives, we can more easily respond in faith to God's loving activity. And we can more easily recognize God's revelation to us in our own lives.

2. People want to learn how to make their lives better. They are not interested in learning what others tell them they should know. They learn as little as possible about what they *have to know* and as much as possible about what they *want to know*.

3. Adults learn differently than children do. The task of children is to acquire facts and to organize them in an orderly fashion. Adults have a vast store of facts and experiences. Their task is not so much to acquire new information as it is to utilize the experiences they have in a way that will help them grow and make their lives happier and more complete.

4. Lectures are the least effective way to help people grow. Active reflection involving both the left and the right sides of the brain, both reason and feelings, both personal experiences and new experiences is the surest and quickest way to help people learn and grow.

5. A learning process involves many elements that come together to help people assimilate new information and change behavior. Adults learn best in situations that allow them to share in the learning process. They have to evaluate their ideas, attitudes, and ways of acting. They have to enlarge, modify, or change their way of thinking. They do this best when they can actively contribute to the learning situation.

6. Sharing in small groups is a powerful tool for building community. One of the most important elements in actively sharing in the learning process is the interaction between the people involved. In a group, sharing the total life experiences of its members, the present perceptions, feelings, and patterns of action of all members are brought to bear on a single point, and out of this intermingling come insights, understanding, acceptance, and change. The outcome is unpredictable. There is no predetermined end product that automatically will be produced, but there is a movement toward something new. This movement to the new involves the total person. It is cognitive, emotional, and physical. Reality becomes bigger than it was before because the participants see it and experience it in a new and different way. This movement toward the new occurs

not only in the participants but also in the facilitator who is attentive to what is occurring in the group.

7. Adults usually do not learn or grow in an orderly, progressive fashion. They learn piecemeal and grow in spurts.
8. Learning and growing spiritually should not be a burden but a zestful and enjoyable journey throughout life.
9. Spiritual growth and human development go hand in hand.

THE SETTING FOR THE ACTIVITIES

The physical and emotional setting in which people get in touch with their stories and share them is most important. A classroom or a large hall with folding chairs is not conducive to interpersonal sharing. A room suited to the size of the group and equipped with comfortable chairs or, for younger people, pillows and carpet is ideal. Name tags, someone to welcome people, coffee, refreshments, and a time for chitchat before the session all help create a hospitable environment.

You can save a lot of time by arranging the chairs before the participants arrive. If possible, place them in a tight circle because it is important for participants to be as close together as possible. If there are too many participants for one circle, form two circles, but do not allow participants to sit in back of the group or away from it. If the activity calls for small group discussions, have a second set of chairs arranged in groups of four or five so no time is lost in realigning chairs. It is usually best to limit the small groups to four or five so that there is adequate time for each person to share.

Many of the activities require the participants to write. If table space for everyone is not available, you may wish to provide large pieces of cardboard that people can hold in their laps and use as a writing surface. Keep in mind that participants should not be seated around tables during discussions but should share in small groups seated in circles.

It is also important to have a comfortable room temperature, adequate light, and proper ventilation so that people do not get drowsy.

The emotional environment is just as important as the physical. The participants need to know one another; therefore, unless they all know one another's names, an icebreaker of some kind should open the sessions. At the beginning of the first few sessions, the participants need to be reassured and reminded that what is shared in the group stays within the group. They also need to be told that they will not be judged, because there are no right or wrong answers to the questions. The activities are not intended to be a tribunal at which one's past life is brought before a jury. Rather, they are intended to promote insight into one's life, as well as acceptance and understanding of one another.

USING THE ACTIVITIES

These activities work best as part of a wider and more complete program. They are especially useful in conjunction with a meeting, a lecture, a day of recollection, or a weekend retreat. They can be used to enhance the content of an RCIA process, or any other form of convert courses, and of programs for youth or young adults. They can be strung together to create a program by themselves. Or they can be used at the beginning and end of a program. The questions and the time allotment will have to be tailored to fit the particular needs of the group.

The group should always be told the reason for using each activity. This reason is spelled out in the "What to Expect" section of the introduction that precedes each of the seven groups of activities, and the facilitator can draw on this section in introducing an activity. When the reasons for the activities are made clear, people who are a bit uneasy about doing the activities or who think of them as childish games will see how they are an integral and important part of a program. Some people feel that the only way to learn is to hear a lecture or presentation of some sort. It will take them a little time to realize how these activities are really learning experiences that facilitate personal growth.

It is important that the group be debriefed about each activity, especially after sharing in small groups. The debriefing should include questions that ask what the participants learned from the activity and how they felt about doing it, as well as a few words from the facilitator explaining how the activity furthers the purpose of the program or of the group.

STRATEGIES FOR CHANGE

The activities are designed to raise consciousness and to help participants discover the patterns of behavior and of thought in their lives. They may also help participants see areas in which they would like to change. The usual reaction after completing one or more of these activities is "How do I move on?" or "Where do I go from here?" Such questions are best answered in the debriefing after an activity or a series of activities. The facilitator will need to decide when and how to answer such questions and what method to use in order to answer them. The facilitator might say, for example, "You have touched on something very meaningful. Perhaps you might expand it a bit for us" or "This is very meaningful to you. Maybe you would like to speak to someone after the session is over" or "Would anyone in the group like to respond?" If it is a very sensitive area or beyond the skills of the facilitator, he or she might want to make a referral.

In general, two approaches are helpful in deciding how to make changes in one's life. The first is based on the premise that change will occur when people see clearly the way in which they think and act and then recognize the need for changing the way they think or act. They will then think differently. Because thoughts change feelings and actions, people will change their feelings and actions by changing their thoughts. Using this approach, people will have to be sure that they see the past clearly and recognize the thinking that has to be changed. In this approach, it is not as necessary to come to a definite action at the end of an activity as it is with the second approach. The change will come about naturally.

The second approach is based on the premise that if people first change the way in which they act, they will change their feelings, attitudes, and way of thinking. If a group decides to use this strategy, the following process for discerning ways to make changes in one's life may prompt some valuable insights. An individual or the whole group could undergo this process at the end of an activity or a series of activities.

1. Brainstorm the options of different ways of thinking or acting.
2. Examine the price of each option and the resources or strengths necessary to carry it out.
3. Arrange the options in order of priority, and pick the one that has the best chance of succeeding.
4. Develop a strategy to carry out the option chosen.
5. Try the option and evaluate it periodically to see whether it is working.

It is not always possible to use the second approach in a short session. It is best used at the end of a day of recollection or at the end of a retreat. In most situations, some combination of both approaches will be used. But in all cases, the participants should see that a better and fuller life is possible for them.

THE ACTIVITIES

The activities in this book can be adapted in any number of ways to fit the needs of a particular group. In most cases, the basic steps of an activity are followed by suggested variations that a facilitator might like to use. The variations are not worked out in as great detail as the basic activity because the facilitator using them will thoroughly understand the basic activity and so will be able to make the necessary adaptations.

Each activity begins with a list of materials needed for that particular activity. These should be collected and ready to use before each session begins.

Several activities include a worksheet or worksheets that are to be duplicated and distributed to all the participants. Each worksheet appears in this book at the end of the activity in which it is used, and permission is given to duplicate these worksheet pages.

THE GROUPS

The activities are intended for groups of adults and of youth who are at least in senior high school. The selection and arrangement of activities is especially geared to parish councils and other small parish groups. If a particular activity works better with one group than it does with others, that fact is noted at the beginning of the activity.

The size of the group will usually be limited only by the facilities available and by the number of people willing to attend. The activities have been used with groups as small as six or eight and as large as four hundred.

In most of the activities, the participants are asked to form small groups that number from four to eight people each. These groups can be formed in any number of ways. The participants can count off or be given cards with the numbers of the groups on them or simply be told to form groups of a certain size. It is a good idea to ask spouses and close friends not to join the same group.

It is suggested that the facilitator make copies of the questions to be discussed in the small groups and give a copy to one person in each group. That person would then ask the questions in his or her group and help keep the discussion on course. In that way, the members of each group can discuss the activity questions at their own pace, independent of the large group.

TIME

Most of the activities are designed to take from sixty to ninety minutes; a few take less time. The age and mixture of the participants as well as the trust level in the group will affect the time needed to complete a given activity. It is important, however, not to run an activity to death. It is best to stop before everything that can be said has been shared. Leave the participants with something to chew on and to think over after they leave the session.

THE FACILITATOR

It is impossible to overemphasize the importance of the facilitator. He or she does not need a great deal of training but must understand the activities and have the goals clearly in mind before the group can effectively and comfortably use the activities. Some time before a session, the facilitator should process the activity to get a grasp on it and to feel the direction in which it is going. In general, the facilitator should follow the instructions closely unless he or she is familiar enough with the activity to make changes without distorting its goal.

The facilitator needs to feel comfortable with silence and not to feel that he or she has to talk when the participants remain silent. Often people need time to formulate their responses. Someone will always break the silence.

The facilitator should give instructions, summarize what has happened, and conduct the debriefing. He or she should have all the materials prepared and ready to distribute before each session begins.

Finally, it is important for the facilitator to realize that he or she is *not* a teacher but a guide and companion. His or her role is to encourage the participants, to promote sharing, and to make sure that everyone is heard and that no one is judged.

1
Paradigms of Change

Life is characterized by patterns of change, or letting go and moving on to something new, of moving from place to place, of dying and rising. Inherent in these patterns are times of crises and uncertainty. The end result is usually a change in one's perception of life and in one's behavior. Often a complete transformation takes place in which new insights develop and form a new structure for a richer way of living and a more Christian way of perceiving reality. Of course, the opposite may also happen; the new that evolves can result in a more cynical approach to life and destructive forms of behavior. Once people recognize this pattern of transition in their lives or in the life of a group, however, they can cope with change in a more productive way.

WHAT TO EXPECT

By using the activities in this chapter, the participants will be able to get in touch with their own histories of change and to see how the changes have affected their lives. The participants will explore some of the key moments in their lives, analyze their patterns of growth, and accept their histories. These insights will lead participants to realize that life is a journey, a dynamic movement. The activities will also help the participants become more aware of the emotional, intellectual, and spiritual content of their lives. This new awareness will create a willingness to look for areas of transition in their lives in order to profit from them.

When the activities are used with groups, the participants will be able to acknowledge that they all have walked similar roads and, it is hoped, will grow in empathy and understanding of other people. The activities will also help the participants accept others who have had different experiences.

Because people are being asked to share what they know best—namely, their own experiences—the activities will spark discussion and will lead people to reflect more deeply on their own life stories in light of the experiences and reflections of the other people in the group. Usually participants will be eager to continue this type of sharing and reflection.

The first three activities present the basic paradigms, or models, of the change process.

- Activity 1, "From Place to Place," outlines four stages that people go through whenever significant changes occur in their lives.
- Activity 2, "Changing through Loss," helps the participants identify and explore six steps that they go through when suffering a significant loss.
- Activity 3, "A Relational Paradigm," outlines four stages in the growth of a significant relationship.

The last three activities are applications of these basic paradigms to Scripture.

- Activity 4, "Stages in the Spiritual Journey," helps the participants examine the various stages in their spiritual development.
- Activity 5, "The Exodus Experience," helps the participants see how they have experienced changes in their vision of life that are similar to the one which the Hebrews experienced in the Exodus.
- Activity 6, "The Paradigms and Scripture Stories," uses Scripture to validate the changes that the participants experience in their lives.

INTENDED AUDIENCE

The activities in this section are most effective with people who have experienced a change in their lives or who feel a need for change. They help lay the foundation for support groups of people who are divorced or grieving, or who have a chemical dependency, because they enable the group members to monitor their progress.

The activities can also be used during retreats and days of recollection, during the RCIA process, and in Scripture classes. They are helpful in marriage enrichment and marriage preparation programs. Groups of parents, teenagers, senior citizens, and members of a parish council can benefit from them as well.

ACTIVITY 1
From Place to Place

This activity outlines four stages that people go through whenever significant changes occur in their lives. By learning to recognize these stages, people can prepare themselves to handle the challenge of transition.

Materials Needed

Name tags (if some members of the group are not acquainted)
A copy of the Activity Worksheet for each participant
Pencils
Variation 2: A story that demonstrates the transition process
Variation 8: A Scripture story that demonstrates the transition
   process

Procedure

Introduce the activity by saying, "This activity will help us identify four stages that we usually go through as we move from place to place in our lives. By recognizing that an inevitable part of living is an orderly process of transition, we become more comfortable with change and can manage it more easily.

"First we will reflect on the process of transition as it occurred when (mention the specific area that the group is concerned with, such as divorce, prayer life, new job). Then we will form small groups and share as much as we feel comfortable sharing with the other members of the group. Afterward, we will debrief ourselves about the activity."

Pass out copies of the Worksheet and run through the four stages briefly. Then ask the participants to fill out the Worksheet, telling them that they have five minutes to jot down their answers. Explain that they need not write the answers out in full. A few words or phrases will do because they are going to tell their stories in the small groups. Make sure, however, that the participants are as specific as possible about what happened at each stage and about their feelings at the time. Also assure them that they need not write something for every stage because they may not have gone through the entire process as yet. For example, a divorced person may not yet have begun to put his or her life together.

After the participants have completed the Worksheet, have them form groups of four or five to share their stories. After each person has had a chance to tell his or her story, ask these questions:

- At the present time, where do you see yourself in this process of transition, and how do you feel about being there?
- What new pattern do you see emerging in your life?
- If you have not completed all the stages, how do you feel about the stages that you have not yet gone through?
- What have you learned so far from going through this process?

After fifteen or twenty minutes, call all the participants together, and debrief them about the activity with these or similar questions:

- What did you learn from hearing the stories of other people?
- How do you think that being conscious of the stages in the process can help you when change is going on in your life?

After everyone has had a chance to share his or her thoughts, close the activity with a spontaneous prayer asking for enlightenment.

Variations

1. *Reinforcing the process.* To reinforce the structure of the process of transition and to give participants a broader view of society at the end of the debriefing, ask the following:

   - Can anyone give an example of this four-step process as it has occurred recently in the Church or in society?
   - What is your evaluation of this change?

2. *Demonstrating the process.* Begin the activity by using a story to show how the process works. Read or tell the story, having the participants point out the places in the story where the transitions occur. Then ask them to use the

Worksheet to write an account of a similar change or transition that took place in their lives. You can use fairy tales such as "Cinderella," "Sleeping Beauty," or "The Ugly Duckling." Or you may wish to use a movie such as *E.T.* or *The Wizard of Oz*. A play such as *Man of La Mancha* or *My Fair Lady* told by a member of the group while the music is being played would also add to the presentation.

3. *Special needs.* For a group of people with special needs such as marital problems, divorce, grief over a death, chemical dependency, or other major life changes, you will need to change the questions to be shared in small groups. After participants have filled out and discussed the Worksheet, they should respond to these or similar questions:

   - When the change or transition occurred, what did you have to leave behind that you wish you could still have?
   - When did you realize that there was no turning back? How did you feel about this?
   - What are some of the obstacles you encounter in sustaining change in your life?
   - Do you see this process at work in some other areas in your life, and how do you feel about it?

   After the groups have shared their feelings and experiences, call the participants together and use the debriefing questions listed in the basic activity.

4. *Parish groups.* Parish councils and other committees or clubs can use this activity to evaluate the changes that have occurred within the group itself or within the parish as a result of the group's work. After the introduction, have the group identify a change in one area that it would like to track—for example, changing from instruction classes for converts to an RCIA process. As a group the participants should use the Worksheet to identify each stage in the process; then debrief the group about the process with questions such as these:

   - What precipitated the change? (Amplify Stage 2.)
   - How did our group and the people of the parish react to the change we wanted to make? What were some of the

difficulties we encountered, and what kind of help did we receive in making the change?

- How is the group (the parish) better off now than it was?
- In what areas of the life of the group (of the parish) do we see the process beginning all over again?

5. *Parent groups.* A group of parents trying to understand their teenage children can use this activity very effectively. After a brief introduction, ask the participants to recall their own teenage years and go through the four stages to identify how they made the transition from childhood to adulthood in such areas as parental authority, relationships, school, and career. Divide the participants into small groups, and have the members of each group share their experiences. Then debrief the entire group about the activity with questions such as these:

- What similarities do you see between what happened in your life and what is going on in the life of your teenager today?
- What were some of the most difficult issues you faced and some of the emotions you experienced? What kinds of help did you find?
- How can we use these insights into our own teenage experiences to build a better relationship with our teenagers?

6. *Families.* Parents and teenagers can do the activity together. Have the teenagers use the Worksheet to chart some transition in their lives, such as going into high school or overcoming some problem. Have the parents chart one of their own teenage transitions, as above in Variation 5. Then have the adults form small groups with an equal number of teenagers to share what they have written. Parents can be teamed with their own teenagers or, if they wish, with other teenagers. Debrief the whole group with questions such as these:

- What transitions were shared in your group?
- What similarities were noted between the experiences the adults had as teenagers and the experiences of the teenagers in the group?

- What kinds of feelings were present in the transitions that were discussed?
- *To adults:* What were some of the most difficult issues you faced as a teenager?
- *To teenagers:* What are some of the most difficult issues you face?
- What things do the adults and the teenagers have in common?
- What did you learn from this discussion?

7. *Ministry.* People in a particular ministry can use the activity to reflect on their personal growth and development through serving others. At Stage 1, have them describe themselves at the beginning of their ministry; then have them go through Stages 2, 3, and 4 to bring to light the changes that have occurred in their lives. In the group discussions, questions like these will prove helpful:

- Why did you enter the ministry, and what did you hope to achieve through it for other people and for yourself?
- What were some of the unforeseen difficulties or problems that came up?
- Where did you find help and support in your efforts?
- In what ways can your experiences help you in your future work?

8. *Bible-study groups.* During a Scripture class, the process can be used to help people see the connection between the lives of people in the Bible and their own lives and to realize that the same process is at work in both cases. Have one person read or tell the story of some character from Scripture, such as Moses, Paul, Abraham, Jesus, Saul, Gideon, or David. Have the group as a whole identify the four stages as they occurred in that person's life, and then have the participants fill out the Worksheet. Debrief the group on the activity with questions such as these:

- What similarities do you see between your life and the life of _____?
- What can we learn from seeing these similarities?
- How can this activity help us better understand Scripture as well as our own struggles?

WORKSHEET
From Place to Place

It is not necessary to fill in the blanks with complete sentences. Write just enough to help you organize your thoughts. You may not have gone through all the stages of the process at this time. Write about only the stages that you know from personal experience.

1. Describe the change or transition that occurred. This might have been an event such as getting your first job, getting married, getting divorced, moving to a new area, or joining the RCIA.

2. *Stage 1—Before the Change.* Your situation may have been good or bad, but it probably was stable; there was a predictable pattern by which you knew what to expect and what was expected of you. In a few words, describe the situation and your feelings before the change.

3. *Stage 2—Key Event.* Something took place that changed or disrupted the predictable, usual pattern. This event marked the beginning of the transition or change. It might have been something that would have been small and insignificant if it had occurred at another time, but in this situation, it proved to be the final straw. Or it might have been a major event in your life. Briefly describe the event that prompted the change.

4. *Stage 3—Confusion.* During the transition time, there was much confusion. Things no longer hung together. You were not sure which way you should go. Even if you had tried to

go back to the old way, it would not have been possible. Describe what went on during this time of confusion and how you felt about it.

5. *Stage 4—New Pattern.* Finally, a new way of acting and being emerged. Things came together again. A new pattern was discernible. This new pattern may not have been either better or worse than the old one, but it was different. Also, it may not have lasted very long because the process of change may have begun once again in some area of your life. Describe how this situation was different from the situation in Stage 1 and how you felt about the new situation.

ACTIVITY 2
Changing through Loss

This activity can be used in conjunction with any one of the transitions or changes that people experience, in order to give them a slightly different view of the process of change. It is particularly effective with people who have suffered a significant loss, such as a divorce, a permanent disability, or the death of a parent, a spouse, or a child.

Materials Needed

Name tags (if necessary)
A copy of the Activity Worksheet for each participant
Pencils

Procedure

Introduce the activity by saying, "Dr. Elisabeth Kübler-Ross outlined five steps that people who are dying usually go through: denial, anger, bargaining, despair, acceptance. These steps can also be used to understand a bit better any change or transition that takes place in one's life. A change from one state to another—for example, from being single to getting married, from going to school to getting a job—involves 'dying' to the first state. This 'little death' often produces the same feelings as those experienced by a person who is actually dying. In designing this activity, the authors have added a sixth step that they have found many people experience—namely, guilt."

Then pass out copies of the Worksheet. Ask each person to identify a change that occurred in his or her life that forced him or her to let go of something important. It may have been the loss of a friendship or merely moving from one city to another. Go over the steps, and have the participants write in their experiences.

When everyone has had time to recall one of these "death-like" experiences, have the participants form groups of four or five and share their answers. After they have shared, have them discuss their responses to these questions:

- What was the most difficult step for you to take?

- When did you come to accept the loss or the change you experienced?
- What help and obstacles did you encounter in making this transition?
- How would you compare the situation you are in now with the one you left behind?

When the groups have finished sharing, call them together and debrief the participants about the activity, using the following questions:

- What have you learned from this activity?
- Do any of you see the process at work in your lives at the present time? If so, and if you feel comfortable, please share your experience with the group.

WORKSHEET
Changing through Loss

It is not necessary to write in complete sentences or with correct spelling and grammar. Just write enough so that you can clearly recall the progression of events and feelings. You may not be able to fill in all the steps because you may not be completely through the process yet.

1. Describe the change or transition in your life.

2. *Step 1—Denial*. People refuse to face the loss or pain and pretend that things are okay. What are some of the things you did to avoid facing the loss? (For example, pretending that everything was all right, overworking, sleeping too much, drinking, taking drugs, becoming sick, being hostile to people, moving too quickly into a new relationship, avoiding friends.)

3. *Step 2—Anger*. People become angry at God, self, or someone else because this is happening. How did you express your anger at the time of the loss?

4. *Step 3—Bargaining*. People try to strike a bargain with fate or God: "If this will not happen, I will do this." What kinds of bargains did you try to strike?

5. *Step 4—Guilt*. People feel responsible for the loss and blame themselves for it. Often these feelings are based on

an unrealistic sense of responsibility. What feelings of guilt did you have?

6. *Step 5—Despair.* Depression, discouragement, and a sense of helplessness set in. What ideas about yourself, others, and the situation kept you from moving on?

7. *Step 6—Acceptance.* In the final step, people accept the change or loss. They acknowledge the pain of the loss, see both the pluses and minuses in what was lost, and recognize that life can and will go on, even though they may continue to feel the loss. What did you do or say that showed you had accepted the loss or change?

ACTIVITY 3
A Relational Paradigm

This is a simple paradigm by which people can examine the growth of a relationship and the changes that have taken place in it. It can be used alone or in conjunction with Activity 1 or Activity 2.

This activity can be used most effectively with married couples to help them examine their years together, with parents looking at their relationship to their children, with priests and religious who are reexamining their vocation, and with converts who have been in the Church for a year or more.

Materials Needed

A copy of the Activity Worksheet for each participant
Pencils

Procedure

Introduce the activity by saying, "All serious relationships develop along more or less the same lines. There is the initial, exciting *discovery* of a person (an institution). After a time comes a period of *disillusionment* as one gets to know the person (the institution) better and finds out that the person (the institution) is not going to meet all one's expectations. Third, there is a period of *redefining* the relationship in terms of the actual reality. Finally, the relationship either dies or one comes to *rediscover* the person (the institution), ending up with a more solid and realistic relationship that is based on true love. In this activity, we will look at our relationship with _____." (Put in the name of the person or institution—for example, "our spouses," "our children," "the parish," "the Church," "the parish council.")

Then pass out copies of the Worksheet. Go over the instructions, and give the participants about eight or nine minutes to complete the Worksheet. Afterward, have the participants form small groups and share their answers to the questions on the Worksheet. (Married couples may wish to share as individuals or as a couple.)

As soon as the discussions begin to wind down, call the groups together and debrief the participants about the activity. Ask the following questions:

- What did you learn from looking at this relationship?
- Do you think you could have arrived at this deep relationship without experiencing any disillusionment and loss?

WORKSHEET
A Relational Paradigm

Write a few words or sentences that will help you organize your memory of what occurred and how you felt at the different stages of the relationship you are exploring. You need not worry about spelling or grammar. In the discussion, you will share only that material with which you are comfortable.

1. Name the relationship that you are going to explore.

2. *Stage 1—Discovery (romance)*. This is the beginning of the relationship. There is a superficial attraction, perhaps even infatuation. Both parties are on their best behavior.

   a. What person or events led to the beginning of the relationship?

   b. What was the initial attraction to the other person (or group or institution)?

   c. Why did you want to have this relationship (or belong to this group)?

   d. What did you say, do, and feel at this time?

e. What did you look forward to as a result of this relationship?

3. *Stage 2—Disillusionment.* The original feeling of enchantment is gone. People are disillusioned as they encounter the reality of the other person. They ask, ''Is this all there is?''

a. What caused you to become disillusioned?

b. How did you feel and act now that the relationship was different?

4. *Stage 3—Redefining the Relationship.* At this point, people can redefine the relationship by letting it quietly die or by trying to rebuild it.

a. What did you do to try to redefine the relationship?

b. Did any person or situation help? How?

c. What were the results of your efforts to redefine the relationship?

5. *Stage 4—Rediscovery (true love).* If the relationship survives, the acceptance of oneself and of the other leads to a rediscovery of the relationship but on a deeper, firmer basis. It is a new relationship based on a truer and more real understanding.

   a. What was the turning point?

   b. How is the relationship different?

   c. How do you feel now that the relationship is different?

ACTIVITY 4
Stages in the Spiritual Journey

Each person has received a special call and has a unique journey that has led him or her to ministry in the Church. For some it has been a long, hard journey with high and low moments. For others it has been relatively easy. This activity will help participants recreate three stages in that journey and learn from them.

Materials Needed

A copy of the Activity Worksheet for each participant
Pencils
A Bible
Variation 2: Substitute Worksheet questions

Procedure

Introduce the activity by saying, "In this activity, we are going to recall the events that led to undertaking our ministry. Then we are going to compare the process we went through with what happened in the life of Jesus when he began his ministry at the moment of his baptism. Jesus realized that his time had come to proclaim publicly the advent of the kingdom of God. Now let's listen to that story from Scripture."

Read Matthew 3:13–17. If you wish, you may use one of the meditation techniques described in Activity 39 to help the participants get into the story.

After the reading, explain what the group is to do: "There are moments in our lives when we see things clearly, as if we are being given a new vision and a new life. Perhaps there was a moment in your life when you decided to take the step toward involvement in the ministry of the Church. Jesus had John the Baptizer to help him. You may have had certain people who invited you, supported you, or helped you in this journey.

"Take a few moments and recall the events that led you to the ministry. Recall the people who helped or encouraged you." (Pause for a moment while the participants recall their stories.)

Pass out copies of the Worksheet and have the participants fill it out. Then have them form groups of three or four and discuss their answers. When the members of the small groups have shared their answers with one another, call them back into the large group and debrief them about the activity with the following questions:

- What similarities and differences did you find in your stories?
- In what way was the process that you experienced similar to the one that Jesus experienced?
- What does this experience suggest to you about the nature of your ministry and where you can go from here?

Variations

1. *RCIA groups.* The same process can be used with a group of people who are interested in joining the Church or in becoming active in it after a period of nonparticipation. Questions such as these might be used in debriefing the large group:

   - What are the similarities and differences in your stories?
   - How is the process that you are going through similar to the one that Jesus went through?
   - What does this experience tell you about the nature of becoming a Catholic?

2. *Parish groups.* The same process, with slightly different questions for each stage, can be used by any parish group to identify how it came into being. The questions to be substituted for those on the Worksheet should be something like these:

   - What was the condition of the parish before our group was established?
   - Why did the parish begin this group?
   - Was there any resistance or were there any surprises in establishing the group?
   - What changes have taken place as a result of our being in existence?

WORKSHEET
Stages in the Spiritual Journey

It is not necessary to write in complete sentences or with correct spelling and grammar. Just write enough so that you can clearly recall the progression of events and your feelings.

1. *Stage 1—Before Joining Ministry.* Describe what your faith world was like before you began your ministry.

2. *Stage 2—Journey That Led to Ministry.* Focus on the moment when you decided to take the step toward involvement in the ministry of the Church.

   a. When did you realize that you were being called?

   b. Who helped you during this period?

   c. What were you feeling during the time of transition?

   d. What resistance to the change did you experience?

   e. What did you have to leave behind?

f. Did you have anything that you could call a mystical experience? If so, describe that experience.

3. *Stage 3—After Joining Ministry.* Focus on the changes that have taken place as a result of your ministry.

a. What did you do to show that you accepted the call to ministry?

b. How did you feel about undertaking your ministry?

c. Were there any temptations to go back?

d. What new challenges do you face in this ministry now?

ACTIVITY 5
The Exodus Experience

This activity helps participants recognize transitions as necessary for human growth. Transitions can come gradually or unexpectedly. They can be gentle or violent. But the essence of these transitions is that people leave one place, one way of seeing reality, one way of living, and move to a new place, a new vision, a new way of living.

Materials Needed

A copy of the Activity Worksheet for each participant
Pencils
A Bible
Variation: Drawing paper and markers, modeling clay, or old
    magazines and glue for a collage

Procedure

Introduce the activity by saying, "Changes often involve struggle and risk. They may be accompanied by feelings of grief because we are leaving the known and of fear because we are entering the unknown. At the beginning, we may deny that the change is happening or that it has happened. We may feel angry, depressed, bitter, resentful. The change may be one we wanted and planned for, or it may be one thrust upon us unwillingly.

"This type of change, or migration from place to place, occurs not only in the lives of individuals but also in the lives of groups of people. The Exodus story in the Bible is the model of all transitions in the lives of individuals and nations. It tells how a people left slavery and found a new and better life in another land. We see in this story the movement from slavery to freedom, from being a nonpeople to becoming a nation, from living in one land to living in a new land."

At this point, you or some well-prepared member of the group should tell the story of the Exodus. The main events are found in Exodus, chapters 3 through 20. Additional material can be found in Numbers and Deuteronomy. Of course, if the participants know the story well, it will not be necessary to retell it. The group could brainstorm the main events of that journey, each person contributing what he or she remembers about the story.

When the story has been told, say, "In our own lives, there have been moments or events that have taken us from some form of bondage to freedom, from one way of life to another. For example, falling in love is one of these turning points, as are finding an entirely different kind of work, getting a divorce, losing a member of the family, converting to a different religion, and taking on a ministry in the Church. All of us have had some kind of transition. Take a few moments to recall one such transition in your life."

Give the group a minute or two to reflect. Then give each person a copy of the Worksheet. Quickly read it over with the group and ask the participants to answer the questions by themselves. When the participants have finished reflecting on the questions, ask them to form small groups of five or six and to share their stories with one another.

Afterward, call all the participants together and debrief them about the activity by asking these questions:

- What were the similarities in your stories?
- How were your journeys like the journey of the Hebrews?
- What do your stories suggest about God's relationship to you?
- What do your stories suggest about the kind of relationship you can have with God?
- What do your stories suggest about life in general and about the direction your lives are taking?

Variation

Reinforcing the experience. Have group members draw either representational or abstract pictures that depict their situations and feelings in each of the three stages shown on the Worksheet. Or, have the participants use clay to mold images that show how they felt at each stage. They might also make collages from pictures in a magazine, illustrating how they felt at each stage in their journey. Then have them share their artwork and answer the debriefing questions listed above.

41

WORKSHEET
The Exodus Experience

It is not necessary to fill in the blanks with complete sentences. Write just enough to help you organize your thoughts. You may not have gone through all the stages of the process at this time. Write about only the stages that you know from personal experience.

1. *Stage 1—Life in Egypt.* Think about what your life was like before you began your journey.

   a. Briefly describe the circumstances of your life before the change.

   b. How did you feel about life, about yourself, and about your relationship to others?

   c. What was the "straw that broke the camel's back" in your case?

2. *Stage 2—Life in the Desert.* Now, reflect on your journey as you began to move toward a new way of living.

   a. What got the transition started? Who was your Moses, or helper?

   b. Was the crossing easy? Why or why not?

c. What emotions did you experience? Was there a Pharaoh breathing down your neck?

d. Did anything unexpected happen that you saw to be an experience of God's love and care for you? If so, describe what happened.

e. What were the pressures and temptations to turn back?

3. *Stage 3—Life in the Promised Land.* You have arrived. Think about what you have learned from your exodus experience.

   a. When you arrived at the new place, what was your new vision of life?

   b. What new strengths did you discover in yourself?

   c. Do you feel that you are better or worse off now than before? Why?

   d. Where do you need an exodus in your life today?

ACTIVITY 6
The Paradigms and Scripture Stories

In using the paradigms of change to share life stories, it is often helpful to begin with a Scripture story and show the paradigm at work in the story before asking people to tell their own personal stories. Activity 1, "From Place to Place," and Activity 3, "A Relational Paradigm," work very well with such stories as the prodigal son, the two disciples on the road to Emmaus, the disciples in the upper room, and the stories of Moses, the Exodus, and Elijah. Whichever story and paradigm you choose, the procedure described below should be used.

Materials Needed

A copy of the Activity Worksheet for each participant
Pencils
A Bible
Variation: Life story of a saint or religious leader

Procedure

Introduce the activity by explaining briefly the paradigm you wish to use and the reasons for using it either to begin a session or to end a session. If you use the activity to end a session, show how the group progressed through the steps of the paradigm during the program or retreat.

Have someone read the story from Scripture, and ask the group to identify the stages or steps in the paradigm. At each step you might ask the participants how they think the main character in the story felt at the time. After the reading, distribute copies of the Worksheet and have the participants fill it out.

Then have the participants form small groups and tell incidents from their lives that are similar to the one just told from Scripture. When the groups are finished sharing, debrief the participants about the activity with the following questions:

- What similarities did you discover between your own stories and the story from Scripture?
- How did this activity help you understand your own life better?

- How did this activity help you understand the Scripture story better?

The examples given below will help you get the most out of whatever Scripture story you use. Feel free to use these as they are or adapt them to your own circumstances.

Example A: The Prodigal Son. After reading the story from Luke 15:11–32, ask the participants to identify the four stages of the paradigm "From Place to Place" in the life of the prodigal son. Distribute copies of the Worksheet and have the participants fill it out. Then have them form small groups and share an incident from their own lives when they have been the prodigal son, the father, or the elder brother. Suggest that they integrate the answers to the following questions as they tell their stories:

- What was going on in your life prior to the event that finally fractured your life?
- What happened?
- What feelings did you experience during the fracture and after it had taken place?
- What did the pain cause you to do?
- How long did the pain last?
- How did you cope with the pain?
- When or how did you come to your senses?
- What occurred in your life similar to the homecoming experienced by the prodigal son?
- Who celebrated with you?
- How has your life changed as a result of this experience?

After the members of the small groups have finished sharing, call them together and debrief the entire group about the activity by asking questions such as these:

- What insights have you gained as a result of this activity?
- How did this activity help you understand your life better?
- How did it help you understand better what Jesus was saying about the heavenly Father?

Example B: The Two Disciples on the Road to Emmaus. The story of two disciples on the road to Emmaus, told in conjunction with "A Relational Paradigm," is an excellent story to use with people who are struggling with the reality of

God or who are returning to the Church after being inactive for some time.

Introduce the activity by saying, "The faith journey of every Christian is summed up in the story of the disciples on the road to Emmaus. At this time, all of us are at some point in that short journey that the disciples took after the death of Jesus. Let's read the story in Luke 24:13–35 and see the various stages they went through."

Read the story, and point out the four stages of the relational paradigm. For the *Discovery* stage ("We were hoping that he was the one who would set Israel free."), discuss how the disciples must have felt when they first encountered Jesus—their high expectations, their enthusiasm—and how they must have felt when they left all in Galilee to pursue a new life with him.

For the *Disillusionment* stage ("Our chief priests and leaders delivered him up to be condemned to death, and crucified him."), discuss how the disciples felt, their sense of loss, their doubts, their reasons for leaving Jerusalem. For the *Redefining* stage ("Were not our hearts burning inside us?"), discuss how the disciples shared their pain with the stranger, who then explained the Scriptures to them. For the *Rediscovery* stage ("They had come to know him in the breaking of the bread."), discuss how the disciples were gradually led to a truer, more realistic vision of Jesus and his mission and how this event affected the rest of their lives.

Then distribute copies of the Worksheet and have the participants fill it out. When the work is completed, have the participants form small groups and share how they too have walked the road to Emmaus. Some people may still be in the Discovery stage, some in the Disillusionment stage. Others may have reached the stage of Rediscovery. Assure them that it is all right to be wherever they are.

When the groups have finished, discuss these questions in the large group:

- How has this activity helped you become more comfortable with what has gone on in your faith life?
- How has it helped you understand the people in the group better?

- What does this activity indicate to you about what may well happen later in your life? How might it help you at that time?

Variation

Sharing life stories. The stories of saints and great religious leaders can be used in a similar way. These people all went through a similar process. Saint Augustine, Saint Ignatius, and Saint Francis of Assisi are fine examples. Even the story of non-Catholic religious leaders such as John Wesley and Martin Luther could be cited. Modern people such as Thomas Merton and Dorothy Day are good contemporary examples. Begin with the story of the disciples on the road to Emmaus, compare it with the story of one of the above-mentioned people, and finally ask the group to talk about their stories. Or simply tell the story of a saint or of a great religious leader, and show how he or she followed this path. Point out the four stages; then ask the participants to tell their own stories.

WORKSHEET
The Paradigms and Scripture Stories

Write only as much of your faith journey as you feel comfortable sharing. Each person is at a different stage in that journey, and he or she may not have reached the final stage of rediscovery yet.

1. *Stage 1—Discovery.* Write about a time in your life when you thought you knew the Lord and walked with him.

2. *Stage 2—Disillusionment.* Think of when and how you lost touch with the Lord. How did this loss come about? What other things were going on in your life at this time? How did you feel about life? about losing the Lord? Did your religious behavior change? If so, how?

3. *Stage 3—Redefining.* Recall your efforts and the events that helped you get in touch with Jesus once more. How did the rebuilding of your relationship with him come about? What did you try to do to rebuild the relationship? What people were involved in your efforts to rebuild the relationship? What role did Scripture, prayer, and the liturgy play in rebuilding your relationship with Jesus?

4. *Stage 4—Rediscovery.* Have you rediscovered Jesus yet? How do you feel about this rediscovery? What new things have you discovered about the Lord? about yourself? Has your religious behavior changed as a result of this rediscovery? If so, how?

2
Charting

We take in information through our senses. We store it, and we have the ability to retrieve what we see, hear, feel, and so on. In some mysterious way, our brains can combine all these bits of information to give us a more complete view of reality, of what really happened in the past, and of the possibilities open to us in the future.

Each person has a favorite way of taking in information and organizing it to represent his or her experiences and view of the world. Some people's favorite method is visual. They take in most easily what they see. They tend to think in pictures and to use visual words in their speech. Other people favor an auditory method. Sounds and talk dominate their personal map of life. Still others, although not a great many, favor their feelings—those impressions that come to them through the sense of touch and their inner kinesthetic sense. Of course, everyone uses all three ways of gathering and organizing information, but each person favors one way or another.

Creating charts will appeal to people whose model of the world is principally visual. It will help them see where they are and where they have been so that they can look forward to where they are going.

In this chapter, there are two basic chart forms used: the life line and the static evaluation graph. Creating a life line is a helpful way for people to get in touch with what is going on in their lives at the present time. By looking at a chronological chart on which they have recorded significant events in their lives, they get a coherent and organized view of their lives. This helps them realize that life is not merely a string of unconnected incidents.

Often people become discouraged in their efforts to grow

spiritually because change occurs so slowly that they do not recognize that they have changed. The life line gives them hope because it helps them see how they have changed and shows that growth and change are possible and are part of the very fabric of life. A chronological chart of some type helps people see the direction in which their lives are going and the patterns that they have developed. Seeing this, people can tap into their abilities and creative powers and use them more effectively.

A static evaluation graph is some sort of bar graph that shows percentages or degrees of how people value certain things or how often they do certain things. This chart form helps people evaluate where they are in their journey through life.

WHAT TO EXPECT

The activities in this chapter provide powerful ways to help people get to know one another and to build mutual support and community because through them people share events that are important to them—events that have shaped their lives and helped make them who and what they are. The charts also create an atmosphere for learning by putting people in touch with their own experiences and opening them to new information that can be helpful to them in their own lives.

- Activity 7, "Creating a Life Line," presents the basic chart, which can be used in many ways.
- Activity 8, "Creating Your Life Dream," helps the participants follow the course of the basic dream that each has for his or her life.
- Activity 9, "Charting the Highs and Lows," presents another way to see the important events in life in a chronological order.
- Activity 10, "Using Bar Graphs," helps people judge the relative importance or influence of things in their lives.
- Activity 11, "Charting the Group's Resources," helps a group identify the resources it has within itself to meet its goals.

- Activity 12, "A Time for Everything," helps the participants decide on the right time to act.
- Activity 13, "Improving Relationships," uses the words of Saint Paul to help people see how they might improve the ways in which they relate to others.

INTENDED AUDIENCE

These activities are very useful during a retreat or day of recollection, when people are examining their lives to find out where they have been and where they hope to go. They are particularly useful for people who have a special problem such as divorce, marital troubles, or drink. But the activities can be used with any group of adults. High school seniors also may be able to use and appreciate the activities.

ACTIVITY 7
Creating a Life Line

There are two basic ways to construct a life line plotting the course of one's life. One way is to draw a line on a large sheet of paper. One end of the line represents birth or some time in the past. The other end of the line represents the present. The line is then divided into periods of one's life, and the important events and people of these periods are written above and below the line.

The other way to construct a life line is to use index cards, one for each period in one's life. This method allows people to record more material and to add to the life line anytime they wish. Whichever way you choose, the procedure is the same.

Materials Needed

A large sheet of paper or several index cards for each
    participant
Pencils
Prayer to the Holy Spirit
Variation 5: A Bible and a candle

Procedure

Introduce the activity by telling the participants that they are going to look at their lives to see the changes that have occurred and to try to discern the direction that their lives have been taking. Ask them to reflect on their lives and to pinpoint the significant periods they have lived through. They may use any criteria they wish to organize their lives. For example, they may choose the jobs they have held or the places they have lived, or they may simply divide their lives into five- or ten-year periods.

Tell the participants to draw a life line and to divide it with small slashes. Then have them write above each section the years covered by that section and the event that signaled the transition from one period to the next. Instruct them to write the high points of that period above the line and the low points below. (If the participants are using index cards, each card represents one period in their lives. They should write the transitional event at the top of the card and the high and low points below.)

When the participants have finished making their life lines, have them form groups of five or six and share the ways in which they divided their lives, the turning points, and the high and low spots. Then tell them to discuss these questions:

- What pattern or patterns do you see in your life line?
- What does your life line tell you about the direction your life is taking?
- How do you feel about your life and its direction or about the patterns that you can discern from the life line?

When the discussions begin to wind down, call the groups together and debrief the participants about the activity by asking these questions:

- How was this activity helpful to you?
- How did it help you get to know the others in the group better?
- What questions would you like to ask about your life line?

Close the activity with a traditional prayer to the Holy Spirit or with a short period of silence for private meditation.

Variations

1. *Particular issue or problem.* When using the life line chart with a group of people who have a particular problem such as divorce or a chemical dependency, or who are concerned with one particular issue such as their relationship with their teenage children, give the same general introduction, but relate it specifically to the problem or issue. Then ask the participants to begin their life line at the point in their lives when they first became conscious of the problem or issue, and proceed from there to the present time, marking out the significant periods and making note of the events in each one. Usually they will identify only two or three periods.

   Then ask the participants to form small groups and to share what they have written. Have them discuss not only how the issue gradually developed in their lives but also what the significant turning points were and how the issue has changed the way in which they see life today.

Afterward, in the large group, the participants may discuss the various ways in which they have dealt with the problem or issue and what they think they should do in the future.

2. *Parish organizations.* Any organization in the parish, such as the parish council, a youth group, or a ministry group, can use this exercise to reflect on its activities over the past year or even over the past several years. While working in small groups, the participants should decide how to divide the periods of time and then, as a group, agree on the significant people and events of those periods. By discussing the items to be placed on the life line, the group will get a good sense of where it has been and of the direction in which it is going.

The small groups should then report to the large group what they have written, and the group should discuss the various reports. The final debriefing might include questions such as these:

- Where has this organization taken us in this period of time?
- Where do we go from here?

3. *Family life.* A family can make a life line or history of the family, listing all the important events in the life of the family—the high points as well as the low points. The parents and children might make their own separate charts and, by sharing them, learn how each sees different things as important or unimportant. Or the whole family together could make the life line, with each person adding the high and low points as he or she sees them. Either method is a helpful way for parents to share with their children the events of their early relationship. For example, they might talk about their courtship, their marriage, their early struggles, the birth of the children, and so on.

4. *Relationship to God.* The life line is particularly helpful for people who are consciously trying to improve their relationship with God by joining the Church, by return-

ing to active participation in the Church, or by seeking to grow spiritually.

Have the participants reflect on their lifelong relationship to God and divide their life lines into periods in which there have been significant changes in that relationship. In each period have them write a few words to note the following: (a) how they pictured God, what they thought about religion, and how their behavior manifested their beliefs; (b) what caused them to change the way they pictured God and to change what they believed and did; (c) the significant people who helped or hindered this change; and (d) the strengths and weaknesses of their different pictures of God.

After the participants have compiled this information, have them share it in groups of four or five. Then, either in small groups or as a large group, ask them to reflect on questions such as these:

- What did you once believe about God that you no longer believe, and why?
- What is one thing that makes you feel good about yourself as you look over this life line?
- What is one thing you feel you have lost as you look over your life line?
- What do you conclude about your relationship to God from the fact that your image of God has changed and may still change?

Note: It is not necessary to plot out one's entire life in order to benefit from this activity. The life line can be used for shorter periods of time—three years, a year, a month, or even a day—to trace how one has encountered God during that period. Looking at only one day can help people see that each day is unique and important.

5. *Models of faith.* Ask the participants to make a life line on which they write in the names of people who have had significant influence on their faith lives—people such as their parents, teachers, priests, and friends. They may also write in a few words telling why each person was significant: for example, "Gave me an appreciation of the Eucharist."

Have the participants form groups of five or six and

share how two or three of the people on their life lines have helped them get to know Christ better.

When the groups have finished sharing, call them all together and say something like, "The history of the People of God is filled with significant people who have been faithful to God's Word and who have passed their faith on to others. They have done this by their example as well as by their teaching. Saint Paul, in his letter to the Hebrews, extols the faith of some of these ancient heroes. He holds up their deeds to help his readers remember who their ancestors in faith were and what they did as people of faith."

Read aloud chapter 11 of the Epistle to the Hebrews. Then ask the participants to go off by themselves and take some time to reflect quietly on how the significant people in their lives helped them grow in faith. After this time of reflection, have the participants write one or two short paragraphs about at least two of these people, following the pattern of Saint Paul: for example, "It was by faith that Joe Smith endured the pains of cancer in his final days. He showed me the meaning of fidelity to God in the midst of great suffering."

When everyone has finished, call the group back together. Form a large circle and dim the lights. Place a lighted candle in the midst of the group. Read aloud Hebrews 11:1–3, and then invite each person to share what he or she has written. Pause between each reading to allow people to assimilate what has been said. End with a spontaneous prayer or song.

6. *Relationship to the Church.* By dividing a life line into periods in which their relationship with the Church changed—for example, as a child, an adolescent, a young adult, or a mature adult—the participants can effectively use the life line to track their relationship with the Church. In each period have them write a few words describing the following: (a) how they felt about the Church and what they did as a member of the Church, (b) events that changed their relationship to the Church, (c) people who had a strong influence—good or bad—on their relationship to the Church, and (d) their feelings right now about being a member of this parish community.

After the participants have constructed their life lines, ask them to form groups of four or five and share the history of their relationship with the Church.

Then call the groups together and debrief them about the activity by asking these questions:

- What do the various stories that you have heard suggest about the course of people's relationship with the Church?
- What do they suggest about the needs people have at different times in their lives?
- What do these stories suggest about reaching out to people who seem alienated from the Church?
- What do they suggest about the kinds of things the parish and this group can do to support people at different periods in their faith journey?

7. *The sacraments.* Introduce the activity by telling the participants that they are going to plot the influence that the various sacraments have had on their lives. (You may pick one sacrament, or you may ask the participants to reflect on all the sacraments they have received. If they reflect on more than one sacrament, it would be better to use index cards rather than a straight line.)

   Tell the participants to use the date that they received the sacrament as the starting point and to break the subsequent time into periods during which there was a change in the way they viewed the sacrament. In each period have them describe the following: (a) how important the sacrament was to them at the time, (b) what caused the change or shift, and (c) some meaningful experiences connected with the sacrament.

   Have the participants form small groups and share what they have written. After the small groups have finished sharing, call all the participants together and debrief them about the activity with questions such as these:

   - In what way have you experienced the reception of the sacraments as an encounter with Christ and with the Christian community?
   - What has this activity revealed about the importance of

the sacraments in people's lives and in the life of the community?

8. *Setting goals.* A simple version of the life line can help a person set goals. Ask the participants to mark the date of their birth at the left end of their life lines and a projected age and year of death at the right end. (Life expectancy is currently a bit more than seventy-five years.) Tell them to put a slash someplace along the line to indicate the present.

Then ask the participants to form groups of four to six. Have each person show his or her life line to the other group members and respond to these questions:

- What have been some of your successes and what do you want to accomplish in the time left to you?
- What contribution have you made to the Church or to society and what contribution do you hope to make in the future?
- What have you done for your family so far and what are some of the things you want to do for your family in your remaining years?

When the group members have finished sharing, ask them to discuss the following questions in light of what they still want to accomplish:

- If you had just one more year to live, in what way would you modify your answers?
- What would you have to change in your present life in order to accomplish your goals?
- What is the first step you need to take in order to put your answers into practice?

Finally, call the groups together and ask the participants to share something Jesus said or did that would confirm or challenge what they need to do if they wish to carry out their goals during their remaining years.

9. *Spiritual direction.* When a person seeks out spiritual direction, it often can be helpful for him or her to create a life line, which shows the significant events in his or her spiritual growth. As new subjects are discussed, he or she can then add material to the life line. For example, one

time the client might trace his or her practice of prayer; another time, the history of a relationship with a particular person. This activity helps both the client and the spiritual director see the movement of God and recognize patterns of behavior in the client's life.

10. *Marriage counseling.* A marriage counselor can ask a couple having difficulty to plot out the high and low points of the relationship, beginning with the date they first met. Each person should make his or her own life line, identifying the events that were turning points in the relationship. Then the couple can compare the life lines and talk about them with the counselor and with each other.

11. *Divorced groups.* The life line in any of its forms is most helpful for groups of divorced people. The debriefing questions should concentrate on how they learned to cope with the changes that came about in the relationship with an ex-spouse. There should also be questions that look to the future and to what the people hope to do with their lives. This activity is very reassuring because it helps people see how well they have managed to cope.

12. *Ministry.* The life line can also be used to help people discover the skills and abilities they have that will be helpful in particular ministries. Ask the participants to divide their life lines according to the various jobs they have held, including their formal schooling. At each period they should write down the jobs they held during that period and the skills that were needed to do the work; for example, "Delivered papers—I learned to be reliable and on time." Make sure that the participants also record the interpersonal skills they have developed, such as listening and being sympathetic to suffering.

Then have the participants form groups of four or five to share their life lines and discuss these questions:

- As you look at your life line, what are some skills you became aware of that you did not know you had?
- How can the skills—the gifts—you have be helpful in the ministry being discussed (or in any ministry)?
- Is there anything new in the present situation that will challenge you to develop new skills?

- What skills do others have that you need at this time? How might you acquire them?

When the groups have finished their discussions, call the participants together and debrief them about the activity with this question:

- Why or how does trying something new and different help you discover the skills and abilities you have and so develop you potential?

ACTIVITY 8
Charting Your Life Dream

Most people have some sort of dream or ambition directing their lives. But sometimes it is hard for people to identify that overall dream or goal. This activity helps participants follow the course of the basic dream that each has for his or her life.

Materials Needed

A large sheet of paper for each participant
Pencils
Variation 2: A Bible for each participant

Procedure

Introduce the activity by saying, "A few people are lucky enough to have developed a conscious dream or goal early in life and to have followed it conscientiously. Most people, however, seem to have different dreams or goals at different times in their lives. Often, when these various goals and ambitions are analyzed, there is a common thread running through them. For example, a person may have held various jobs in seemingly different fields, but all of them in some way or another involved helping people. Helping others, then, would be that person's overriding dream or goal. In this activity, we will try to discern the dreams or goals that have been directing our lives. At times, we may not have been conscious of them, but we hope that by seeing the progression of goals in our lives, we will be able to identify dreams." (If you have worked out your own life dream, it would be helpful to use it as an example for the group.)

Ask the participants to make a life line and to divide it into various periods. Have them write in the dreams or goals they have had during each period. To help them see that they have had different dreams or goals, have them ask themselves, "What did I expect or want out of life when I was eighteen or twenty-five or thirty-five or forty-five and at the present?" Or have them ask themselves, "What was the question I asked of life at these various periods in my life, and what were the questions life asked of me?"

Then have the participants form small groups and share their life lines of dreams. After they have shared, they should discuss these questions:

- At each stage in your life, were you living out your own dream, or were you trying to live up to other people's expectations of you?
- How did you feel about what you were doing?
- As you look back at the dreams or goals that guided you at each stage of your life, do you see some sort of thread or overall dream running through them?
- If you are not fully living your own dream or goals that guided you at each stage of your life, do you see some sort of thread or overall dream running through them?
- If you are not fully living your own dream at present, what prevents you from realizing your dream? Are these barriers real or imaginary?

When the groups have finished, call all the participants together and debrief them about the activity with questions such as these:

- How did you feel about doing this activity?
- What did you learn about yourself and others from this activity?
- What do you think you can do now to realize your dream more fully?

Variations

1. *Role of a mentor.* When the participants state their dreams or goals for each period of life, ask them to identify the mentor they had during that period. Then have them discuss these questions:

   - In what aspect of your life did you need a mentor or find one helpful?
   - At what point did you feel that you no longer needed your mentor?
   - How do you feel about losing or pulling away from your mentor?

2. *Using Scripture.* Have each participant select a passage
   from Scripture, either a few verses or a story, that expresses
   his or her dream. Then have all the participants share their
   responses to these questions:

   - How does the passage express your dream?
   - How do you see the dream taking shape in your life?
   - How do you feel about the dream at this time in your
     life?

ACTIVITY 9
Charting the Highs and Lows

Another way of using a chart to get in touch with one's story is to have participants pinpoint on a graph those events that were high points and those that were low points. This activity will work best if participants chart the course of just one area of life—ministry, prayer, marriage, relationship to God or the Church, and the like. The reflection questions should then be tailored to suit the area that is being charted.

Materials Needed

A copy of the Activity Worksheet for each participant
Pencils

Procedure

Introduce the activity by telling the participants that the Worksheet will help them get in touch with what has been going on in their lives. Then pass out a copy of the Worksheet to each participant, and read the instructions aloud. After handling any questions from the group, have the participants complete the exercise in silence.

When the participants have finished, have them form small groups to share their charts. In this sharing they should discuss questions such as these:

- What have you learned from this visual representation of your life?
- What was the lowest point in your life? Explain.
- How did you come out of that low point?
- What was the highest point in your life? Explain.
- Where are you right now?
- What does this chart tell you about the direction your life is taking?

When the small-group discussions begin to wind down, call the participants together and debrief them by asking:

- Does it help you to see your life in a visual way? If so, how?
- How has this activity helped you get more in touch with your life?

WORKSHEET
Charting the Highs and the Lows

In the space below, briefly describe four or five events in your life that you consider to be high points. To the right of each description, write down the year in which the event occurred.

High Points   *Year*

Now, in the space below, briefly describe four or five events that you view as low points in your life. Don't forget to write down the appropriate year.

Low Points   *Year*

Look at the chart on the following page. Use the information you have just recorded to plot the highs and lows of your life. First, fill out the year line. At the beginning of the line, write the year of your birth, and then, depending on your age, fill in every fifth or tenth year following your birth. Second, place a dot above the line for each year in which you experienced a high point, and a dot below the line for each year in which you experienced a low point. Where you place the dot should show how high or how low this experience was for you. A 5 means "very high" or "very low." A 1 means "somewhat high'' or ''somewhat low.'' Third, connect all of the dots on the chart by drawing one continuous line. Begin the line at the year of your birth.

5

4

3

2

1

_____

   19__   19__   19__   19__   19__   19__   19__

1

2

3

4

5

ACTIVITY 10
Using Bar Graphs

A graph provides an excellent way for people to put different aspects of their lives in perspective. In this activity, the participants use a bar graph to see how well they live each of the Beatitudes and to determine in which areas they need further improvement. This same activity can be used with any of the lists in Scripture that enumerate different qualities that the People of God have.

Materials Needed

A Bible
A sheet of newsprint and a felt-tip pen for each group
Masking tape
A copy of the Activity Worksheet for each participant
Pencils or crayons

Procedure

Introduce the activity by explaining the importance of charting one's spiritual progress. Tell the group that a bar graph is one way in which people can obtain a picture of their growth, compare and measure different aspects of this growth, and see where improvement is needed. Inform the participants that they will use a bar graph to chart their progress in living the Beatitudes.

First, ask the participants to form eight groups with an equal number of people in each group. Assign each group one of the Beatitudes. (See Matthew 5:3–11 for a complete list of the Beatitudes.) Ask each group to choose a reporter.

Inform the groups that they each represent an evaluation committee. Their task is to establish criteria for evaluating a person's performance on the Beatitude assigned to the group. They are to accomplish this task by brainstorming actions a person would perform to be considered excellent in this area. Review the process of brainstorming by saying, "The purpose of brainstorming is to allow a spontaneous outpouring of ideas from each member of the group. It is not a time to analyze each idea. It is a time to list each idea suggested." The reporter is to list each suggestion on the newsprint. After the group has exhausted its list, the group is to suggest a person in Scripture (other than Jesus) or in the history of the Church who particularly manifested the Beatitude and write that person's name at the bottom of the list as a star example.

When the groups have finished this task, ask each reporter to present his or her group's list and then tape the list to the wall where it can be seen by everyone.

Next, distribute the Activity Worksheet to each participant. Ask the participants if they have ever used or made a bar graph. If there is anyone in the group who has never seen a bar graph, have someone else in the group explain how a bar graph is used. Then read through the instructions on the Worksheet. Ask the participants to use the criteria established by the groups to help them evaluate themselves. Remind them that the lists are merely guidelines to help them. They are not competing with anyone else. They are examining their own progress to see where they might need improvement and to affirm themselves in areas where they have excelled. Give each participant a pencil or different colored crayons to fill out his or her chart.

When the participants have finished their bar graphs, have them form small groups of four to six. Ask the participants to share with the group the highest rated items on their graphs and to explain why they rated themselves well on this Beatitude. Then ask them to share their answers to these questions:

- How is this quality active in your life?
- In which area do you particularly need to grow, and what is one thing you can do to grow in this area?
- How can this group help you in your effort?

If members of the group know each other well, it may be helpful to have each person point out the two or three highest rated qualities he or she has observed in the other group members. The person should also mention when and how these qualities have been manifested.

Call the groups together and debrief the participants about the activity with questions such as these:

- What does the fact that you do not have all these gifts to the same degree suggest to you about yourself, about your rela-

tionship to God and to your neighbor, and about your be-
longing to a community?
- How did you feel about rating yourself? What benefits do
  you see in this kind of activity? What are the pitfalls?
- What does the fact that each of us has these qualities in
  different degrees suggest about our living and working together in community?

Variations

1. *Other self-evaluations.* The bar graph can be used to explore other qualities that the People of God are expected to
   have, for example, the gifts of the Holy Spirit (*see* Isaiah
   11:2–3), Paul's description of love (*see* 1 Corinthians 13:4–
   7), or the fruits of the Holy Spirit (*see* Galatians 5:22–23).
2. *Prioritizing.* Have the participants rank the qualities, putting the ones they feel they possess most fully at the top of
   their lists and the ones they feel they possess least at the
   bottom of their lists. Have the participants discuss why
   they chose a particular order.

WORKSHEET
Using Bar Graphs

Use the bar graph shown below to measure and compare how well you live the Beatitudes. Consider the criteria for excellence set in the small groups and then fill in each bar to the degree that you recognize the Beatitude in your life. Use the keys to help you complete the graph.

Horizontal Key

1 = "poor in spirit"
2 = "sorrowing"
3 = "lowly"
4 = "hunger and thirst"

5 = "shows mercy"
6 = "single-hearted"
7 = "peacemakers"
8 = "persecuted"

Vertical Key

A = Excellent, consistently present
B = Very good, not always consistent
C = Average, room for improvement
D = Very weak, needs much improvement
F = Nonexistent

ACTIVITY 11
Charting the Group's Resources

This activity helps the participants develop a list of possible projects and identify the personal resources available within the group that will contribute to the success of the projects. The activity also elicits a commitment from the participants to use their skills and abilities in meeting the group's final goal.

Materials Needed

Two sheets of newsprint or a display board
A copy of the Activity Worksheet for each participant
Pencils
A colored pen and two self-adhesive name tags for each participant
Variation 1: Newsprint or a display board
Variation 2: Newsprint or a display board, and a sheet of paper for each participant

Procedure

Introduce the activity by saying, "We have been thinking about doing some project as a group. This activity will help us determine what we might like to do, and more important, it will help us identify the skills and talents we have to carry out our project. Among us we have many talents and resources. Some of these may currently be hidden from us. Others may be more readily apparent. Still others may be obvious, but perhaps we don't see them as helpful."

As a first step have the group brainstorm projects that need to be done. As the participants call out the projects, list them on a large sheet of newsprint or on a display board. There should be no discussion of the relative merits of the projects or of their practicality until all suggestions have been listed. Then spend a brief time discussing the value of each project, what would be needed to carry it out, and what the obstacles might be. After the discussion, have the group vote on the three most promising projects. Tally the votes, and post the results on another large sheet of newsprint or on a display board.

Then distribute copies of the Worksheet and ask participants to complete the exercise. After everyone has marked his or her Worksheet, have the participants gather in groups of five or six. The participants should take turns describing their two best qualities and how they can use these qualities to help the group complete one of the projects.

When the groups have finished sharing, give each person a colored pen and two self-adhesive name tags. The participants should print the following information on each tag: name and one or two words describing his or her two best qualities. Then each participant should stick the name tags on the chart next to the projects that will benefit the most from the participant's talents.

After the participants have positioned their tags, have the group analyze the three projects to see which one is the most feasible based on resources, time, support, and follow-up. Be sure to keep the discussion specific and practical. Once the group reaches a consensus, allow the participants time to determine how the details of the project will be handled. During this planning stage, everyone should be made to feel needed and that his or her contribution is important.

Variations

1. *Tailoring the group's resources.* After the participants have reached a consensus on what project they would like to do, have the group brainstorm the skills and personal qualities that are needed to complete the project. As the participants call out their ideas, write them down on a large sheet of newsprint or a display board. Then have the group weed out the list for the eight most important skills and personal qualities. Give each participant an opportunity to tell what he or she can contribute in terms of the list. Afterward, the group can decide on how best to use the group's resources in completing the project. If a particular project needs someone with a specialized skill, suggest that the group invite an outside support person to help on the project.
2. *Using Scripture.* Another way to discover the participants' personal qualities is to examine Saint Paul's description of love in 1 Corinthians 13:4–8 and to see how these qualities

exist in the group. Introduce the activity by saying, "We are going to do an exercise to help us assess the personal qualities of the group. We all have different abilities, and we all have developed to different degrees the qualities of love that Saint Paul described. This exercise is in no way judgmental; we are merely looking for the best in each person so that we can utilize our resources to the maximum."

Then print on a large sheet of newsprint or on a display board the word *Love* and the following list of characteristics:

is patient	does not brood over injuries
is not jealous	rejoices with the truth
does not put on airs	is not forbearing
is not snobbish	is trusting
is never rude	is hopeful
is not self-seeking	is enduring
is not prone to anger	is unfailing

Tell the group to study the list, and then have each participant write down the three characteristics which would best describe his or her attitudes and actions. The participant should then select one of these characteristics and share the answer with the group, giving an example of how he or she manifests this quality in everyday life. Finally, the participant should tell how having this quality will help him or her meet the needs of the group.

3. *Using the Worksheet.* The Worksheet can be used as a tool to learn more about oneself, even without brainstorming any projects. Have the participants complete the Worksheet and then share the results with the group, giving examples of how they try to practice their best qualities. After each participant has shared his or her answers, the group should provide some feedback on the participant's presentation. Remind the group that the key words during this activity are *kindness* and *gentleness*.

WORKSHEET
Charting the Group's Resources

Below is a list of qualities that Saint Paul says are the fruits of the Holy Spirit's presence in your life (see Galatians 5:22–23). Read each of the descriptions. Then rate each from 1 to 6. The number *1* means "I possess this quality to a very strong degree," and the number 6 means "I do not possess this quality at all." The other numbers show shades in between.

1. Love (giving, caring, sensitive to others)

    1   2   3   4   5   6

2. Joy (exuberant, sunny, cheerful)

    1   2   3   4   5   6

3. Peace (quiet, inner security, in harmony with God and self)

    1   2   3   4   5   6

4. Patience (enduring trying situations, exhibiting staying power)

    1   2   3   4   5   6

5. Kindness (warmhearted, gracious, helpful)

    1   2   3   4   5   6

6. Generosity (open, willing to share)

    1   2   3   4   5   6

7. Faith (never forgets a friend, always there when needed)

    1   2   3   4   5   6

8. Mildness (strength wrapped in understanding and tenderness)

    1   2   3   4   5   6

9. Chastity (cool and stable, resistant to pressure, truthful)

    1   2   3   4   5   6

ACTIVITY 12
A Time for Everything

This activity helps participants learn how to make decisions a little better by looking at the consequences and costs of each decision they make.

Materials Needed

A Bible
A copy of the Activity Worksheet for each participant
Pencils

Procedure

Introduce the activity by asking the participants to close their eyes and listen quietly as you read aloud Ecclesiastes 3:1-8. After the reading, say, "In the Bible passage you just heard, the writer tells us that there is a right time for each thing we have to do. This right time can best be judged by what we hope to gain and what we have to lose once we make a decision. In order to lead a balanced life, it is important to recognize that life is made up of many movements in which we put something aside and take up something else. Good and helpful things we do today may not be good and helpful tomorrow and vice versa. We can usually see this process at work in big decisions, like whether to move on to college or to the working world after high school graduation. It is not always so easy to see the process in smaller decisions, such as volunteering to do a job for a church organization or getting involved in a ministry."

Then distribute copies of the Worksheet, and have the participants complete "The Decision" section. Emphasize that the decision need not be a big decision; it can be any of the smaller decisions that people face all the time. For example, a high school girl may be faced with the decision of whether or not to try out for cheerleading; she has two options—to try or not to try.

After everyone has finished writing, briefly explain the second part of the Worksheet. Point out that in each decision one makes, something is left behind and something new takes its place. The phrases from Ecclesiastes will help the participants analyze what is involved in the decisions they are facing.

When the participants have finished filling out the Worksheet, have them form small groups and share their remarks. Encourage the groups to allow open debate and discussion on the ideas that are presented. Afterward, gather all the participants together and debrief them about the activity by asking the following questions:

- What did you learn from this activity?
- How do you think an activity like this can help you face difficult situations or hard decisions in the future?

WORKSHEET
A Time for Everything

The Decision. Read the two questions below and then briefly describe the decision you are facing and the options open to you. Remember, it is not necessary to write in complete sentences. After you complete this section, do not continue any further until you are told to do so.

1. What is the decision that you are facing?

2. What options do you see open to you?

Analyzing the Decision. Jot down a brief answer to each question below. See if your answers help clarify the best option for you in making your decision.

1. "A time to be born, and a time to die."

   a. In the decision, what is dying or coming to an end?

   b. What is coming to life or beginning to happen?

2. "A time to tear down, and a time to build."

   a. Are there any obstacles to remove?

    b. What steps can you take to move things forward?

3. "A time to weep, and a time to dance."
    a. How do you feel about letting go of what was?

    b. Are there any feelings of expectation or joy? Describe.

4. "A time to keep, and a time to cast away."
    a. Is there anything of the past that you need to hang on to?

    b. What of the past must be put aside?

5. "A time of war, and a time of peace."
    a. What turmoil are you experiencing?

b. How does peace seem possible?

6. Which option seems most appropriate in light of your answers?

ACTIVITY 13
Improving Relationships

This activity helps the participants review their attitudes about relationships in general and explore ways they can improve their present relationships.

Materials Needed

A Bible
A copy of the Activity Worksheet for each participant
An index card for each participant
Pencils

Procedure

Introduce the activity by saying, "Almost everyone has at least one personal relationship that he or she would like to improve. One way people sometimes try is to concentrate on the negative—'I'm going to *stop* doing such and such.' But a much more profitable way is to analyze the qualities of a good relationship and then try to emulate those qualities. For example, in a healthy and strong relationship, how do the people treat each other? How do they speak to each other? How do they help each other in times of trouble? How do they have fun together? Often we will find that before we can do better, one or more of our basic attitudes toward the other person will have to change. Let's use Saint Paul's exhortations from Romans 12:9–21 to explore our attitudes so that we can make one of our good relationships even better."

Read Romans 12:9–21 to the group. Then pass out a copy of the Worksheet and an index card to each person. After the participants have finished writing, have them choose one item on the Worksheet which they have given a low rating and copy that item on the index card in question form; for example, "How can I improve my ability to be generous in offering hospitality?"

When they have finished, ask the participants to form small groups and to place their index cards face down in the middle of the group. Tell the participants to discuss the relationships that they considered when filling out the Worksheet. Point out that they should share only those items that they rated with a 1 or 2 on the Worksheet.

Then, when everyone in a group has shared, have each person pick up a card and, one at a time, answer the question on the card. Anyone receiving his or her own card should not acknowledge that fact.

When the discussions begin to wind down, call the groups together and debrief the participants about the activity by asking the following questions:

- How was this activity helpful to you?
- Do you see any changes you need to make in your relationships?
- What other ways can we use Scripture to help us improve our lives?

Conclude the activity by rereading the selection from Romans and by praying spontaneously.

WORKSHEET
Improving Relationships

Below is a list of the actions Saint Paul recommends for maintaining good relationships (see Romans 12:9–21). Think of a relationship that you would like to improve, preferably a relationship which is good for you. Read each of the descriptions below. Then rate each from 1 to 6. The number 1 means "I do this with great frequency," and the number 6 means "I never do this." The other numbers show shades in between.

1. Anticipate each other in showing respect.

    1   2   3   4   5   6

2. Rejoice in hope.

    1   2   3   4   5   6

3. Persevere in prayer.

    1   2   3   4   5   6

4. Look on the needs of others as your own.

    1   2   3   4   5   6

5. Be generous in offering hospitality.

    1   2   3   4   5   6

6. Have the same attitude toward all.

    1   2   3   4   5   6

7. Live peaceably with everyone.

    1   2   3   4   5   6

8. Do not avenge yourself.

    1   2   3   4   5   6

9. Feed the hungry, give drink to the thirsty.

    1   2   3   4   5   6

3

Using Images

Studies have shown that the human brain has two learning centers—the left side, or the logical side, and the right side, or the creative side. The logical side causes us to think in linear ways, using concepts and giving rational answers. The creative side causes us to think in ways that encompass feelings and experiences, giving visual images and impressions. The right side of the brain views things in the present. The left side, on the other hand, is very aware of the past, the present, and the future.

Ordinarily we are not taught to think *holistically*—that is, using both sides of the brain. Rather, we are taught to use the left side, analyzing bits and pieces of information about a certain subject. To tap our full potential, however, we must learn to use both the left and the right sides of the brain.

Recent studies have shown that images (which come from the right side of the brain), rather than concepts, tend to form people's religious practices and attitudes. To achieve spiritual growth, therefore, it is important to keep from relying solely on the left, or rational, side of the brain and instead to tap the brain's full powers by using both the left and the right sides.

The activities in this section engage the creative side of the brain by having the participants describe their images, feelings, and experiences.

WHAT TO EXPECT

Through the activities in this chapter, the participants will find new ways of getting in touch with their religious experiences. They will be provided with visual ways of assessing the present quality of their lives, and as a result they will become clearer about their relationships with God, Jesus, and the Church. As sharing takes place, they will clarify their own perceptions and gain insights into how others see the same realities. These activities will enable people to understand themselves better and to grow in acceptance of others who may process information differently. Using these activities in a group will also engender a better spirit of community and cooperation among the participants as they share their own special views.

- Activity 14, "Map of Life," helps the participants create a map of their present life.
- Activity 15, "Personal Images of God," explores how the participants picture God.
- Activity 16, "House of God," explores the various images of God projected by the church building in the parish.
- Activity 17, "Images of God in Scripture," helps the participants grasp the meaning of various scriptural images of God.
- Activity 18, "The God Bag," uses magazine pictures to help the participants clarify their operative images of God.
- Activity 19, "Images of the Church," breaks open some of the many images of the Church used in the documents of Vatican II.
- Activity 20, "Creating a Model of the Church," guides the participants in building a model of their vision of the Church.
- Activity 21, "Picture Study," gives the participants a process by which they can look at photos and discover what the pictures say about their lives.
- Activity 22, "Pictures of Jesus," shows Jesus in his various roles to help the participants clarify their image of him.

INTENDED AUDIENCE

The following activities will work well with a variety of individuals and groups. They will be especially meaningful to groups of individuals whose inner lives are in confusion because of conflicting feelings and ideas about God, Jesus, or the Church.

The activities can be used with groups of people of differing ages, such as adults and teenagers or adults of different generations. They are especially helpful with such groups as parish councils, liturgy teams, and parish staffs in which people often have different visions of God, Jesus, or the Church. Through these activities, group members will come to understand how other people perceive these realities.

ACTIVITY 14
Map of Life

There is an intimate connection between internal and external realities. By drawing images of their interior lives, the participants will discover how their inner lives impact upon outer realities. This activity helps people unify different aspects of their lives, making their inner convictions more congruent with their external behavior.

Materials Needed

A large sheet of drawing paper or newsprint for each participant
Different colored crayons or markers

Procedure

Introduce the activity by saying, "Today we will try to isolate various aspects of our interior lives by drawing maps. These will not be road maps but topographical maps, which show hills, valleys, bodies of water, deserts, plains, and so on. Each feature we put on our maps will represent some aspect of our lives at present. For example, a desert might symbolize a feeling of dryness and of being distant from God, a mountain might symbolize the lofty feeling of being in love, and a forest might show a confusion about a career choice." (At this point, it would be helpful to show the group a map of your present state of mind and explain what the various features symbolize.)

Assure the participants that they do not have to be artists to draw the maps. Any way they choose to draw the various features on the map will do. Suggest that they choose the colors of the crayons or markers which symbolize their state of being. For example, a black stormy sea might show that the person is in a state of turmoil over a strained relationship, while a clear blue lake might represent the peace and calm the person finds through listening to music. Ask the participants to reflect for a few moments and then allow their imaginations to go to work. Explain that very often when one begins to draw, ideas will start to emerge.

Give each person a large sheet of drawing paper or newsprint, and have several sets of crayons or colored markers available. Tell the participants that they have ten minutes to draw their maps. Two or three people can share the same set of markers or crayons. Move from person to person, encouraging the participants in their efforts to draw and answering any questions they may have.

When everyone has finished drawing, have the participants form groups of four or five and share their maps with one another. As each person holds up his or her map, the other group members should try to guess what the items on the map represent. After everyone has had a chance to give an opinion, the person holding the map should explain what he or she intended to portray.

After the members of the small groups have shared and explained their maps, have them discuss the following questions:

- What does your map tell about your present life?
- What is your overall feeling about your life map?
- How would you want to change your map?
- Where is the best terrain for development on your map, and where is the poorest?

Call the groups together and debrief the participants about the activity by asking:

- How did you feel while doing this activity?
- What did you learn about yourself from doing this activity?
- How has this activity helped you determine the state of your religious life?

Variation

Sketching a floor plan. Instead of having the participants draw maps, ask them to sketch floor plans of a shopping mall. Instruct them to draw a floor plan of different types and sizes of stores in the mall. Each store should represent a different aspect of their lives, and the size of each store should indicate the relative importance of some item in their lives. For example, a small bookstore would show that reading and education

TOUCHSTONE

do not have too much importance in their lives, but a large music store would show that they love music and that it is important to them.

In small groups the participants could discuss questions similar to those suggested above. The discussion would then be followed by a debriefing process similar to the one suggested above.

ACTIVITY 15
Personal Images of God

The reality of the person of God is greater than anyone can comprehend or experience. Scripture uses images such as Father, Lord, rock, shepherd, and warrior to describe the greatness of God. This activity will help participants explore their own mental images of God and see how these images affect their relationship to God.

Materials Needed

Modeling clay, pipe cleaners, drawing paper, and crayons
Variation 1: Enough art material for each participant to create three or four images
Variation 2: Drawing paper and crayons

Procedure

Introduce the activity by saying, "We can all describe God in philosophical or theological terms: God is a spirit, God is all-powerful, and so on. What we will try to do in this activity is picture God in concrete images rather than describe God in abstract words, so that we can work toward developing a clear mental picture of God."

Have the participants close their eyes and relax. Invite them to picture God in their minds. Give them about two minutes for this. Then make available modeling clay, pipe cleaners, drawing paper, and crayons. Tell the participants to draw or create the image of God that came to mind when they tried to picture God. If some of the participants choose to draw, encourage them to use colors which express both their ideas and feelings about God.

Have the participants form small groups and share their creations with one another. When they have shared their images, have them discuss these or similar questions:

- What does your image say about your thoughts and feelings about God?
- How does your image of God influence the way you pray and act?

- How does your image of God affect your thoughts and feelings about yourself?
- Does your image of God reflect your parents in any way?
- What do you do that projects your image of God to others? For example, if you see God as a judge, are you, in turn, judgmental?
- In what way would you like to change your present image of God?

When the groups have finished their discussions, call all the participants together and debrief them about the activity by asking the following:

- How does the fact that everyone has a different image of God affect the way you would communicate your faith to others?
- How do the differing images of God affect the way people pray together?
- How are your expectations of God and of the Church influenced by your image of God?

Variations

1. *Changing images of God.* Instead of having the participants create only their present images of God, give them enough materials to create three or four images. Each image should show how the participant experienced God at different times in his or her life. For example, you can ask the participants to represent how they pictured God when they were children, when they were in their teens, and when they were going through a time of sorrow.

   Have the participants form groups of four or five to share their images and discuss these questions:

   - How did these various images of God affect the way you thought and felt about God? the way you prayed and acted?
   - From whom do you think you got those images?
   - What happened in your life to create any changes in the way you imaged God?

After everyone has had a chance to share, call the small groups together and debrief them by asking the following:

- How have the changes in your image of God affected what you believe about God and how you talk about God to others?
- How have these changes affected how you feel about the Church?
- How do you feel about the fact that your present image of God may change in the future?

2. *Parish groups.* The parish council, a liturgy team, or the parish staff might take some time at a meeting to have each person draw his or her image of God. Each person should then share his or her image with the entire group. During this sharing, no one should comment or ask questions. Then the group should discuss questions such as these:

- What does the fact that we hold different images of God mean for the group and its work?
- What does the fact that different people in the parish hold different images of God mean for the work of our group?

ACTIVITY 16
House of God

Every church building reflects an image of God in the way it is constructed, how it is laid out, what art and other decorations are displayed. This activity is designed to help the participants explore the image of God projected by their church building. It will work well with the parish staff, liturgy team, or with any organization in the parish.

Materials Needed

A sheet of paper and a pencil for each participant

Procedure

Take the participants on a walk around the outside of the church building as well as inside the church. Before they begin their walk, instruct them to walk around in silence, getting a "feel" for the place. At the end of the walk, go back to your meeting room. Tell the participants to find a comfortable place to sit but to allow ample space between each other. Then distribute sheets of paper and pencils. Ask the participants to write about how they see God reflected in the following aspects of the church: the shape of the building, the design of the interior and exterior of the building, the decorations, the seating arrangement, the symbols, and the sanctuary.

When the participants have finished writing, gather them together in a group and ask them to share their reflections. Then debrief the group by asking the following questions:

- What is the primary image that our church building projects?
- What image do we want our building to project?
- Do we need to make any changes to project the desired image?
- What have you learned from this activity?

Variation

The liturgy. Have the group attend a Sunday liturgy. Instruct them in advance to notice what image of God is projected in each of the following areas: hospitality, music, the readings, the homily, communal participation, the decorations, and the various ministers (including the celebrant, altar servers, lectors, cantors, musicians, and Eucharistic ministers).

Bring the group together after the liturgy to discuss their findings. Ask the following:

- What image of God is the primary image of our faith community?
- How is this image reflected in the lives of our people?
- Is change desirable? If so, how can it be brought about?
- What have you learned from this experience?

ACTIVITY 17
Images of God in Scripture

This activity may be used by Scripture study groups to help the participants explore the various images of God found in Scripture. This activity is also appropriate for RCIA and Confirmation groups.

Materials Needed

A rock for each participant
A Bible
Background music

Procedure

Introduce the activity by saying, "There are many different images of God in Scripture. Each one tries to convey some small aspect of that reality which cannot be comprehended by the human mind and which cannot be put into words. One of these images is God as our rock. In this activity, we will examine a rock to see what the qualities of a rock suggest to us about some aspect or trait of God."

Give each person a rock. As you distribute the rocks, tell the participants to examine their rocks closely and to think about how they would answer these questions: "What does your rock look like? How does it feel? How could you use a rock to support you? to protect you?" Then read aloud the following Scripture passage: "O Lord, my rock, my fortress, my deliverer, my God, my rock of refuge!" (2 Samuel 22:2). Explain that David sang these words when God had rescued him from the hands of Saul. Then give the group some time to reflect on the image of God as a "rock of refuge." If possible, play some appropriate background music during the reflection period.

Before the participants become too restless, ask them to set aside their rocks and discuss the following questions:

- What are the qualities of a rock?
- Why do you think David called God his "rock of refuge"?
- In what way is God your "rock"?
- How can you share this image of God with others?

Close with a spontaneous prayer or a litany. Try to include in the prayer all the characteristics of God that have been discussed. If the participants know one another fairly well, you may want to have them tell how each member of the group mirrors the Godlike qualities of a rock.

Variation

Other scriptural images. This activity may be used with any of the many images of God found in Scripture. It might be good to discuss several of those images, one at a time, over an extended period. These images would include: light (Psalm 27:1), lover (1 John 4:16–19), potter (Jeremiah 18:1–6), buried treasure (Matthew 13:44–46), word (Isaiah 55:10–11), tree (Sirach 24:13–21), sweet fragrance (Song of Songs 1:12–14), wrestler (Genesis 32:23–31), strong wind (Acts 2:1–2), and gentle breeze (1 Kings 19:9–3).

ACTIVITY 18
The God Bag

The way in which a person "sees" God depends on many different factors. One of these factors is personal experience. Another is the example of others. Still another is what one is taught to believe by parents, catechists, or pastors. This activity helps the participants discover the roots of their images of God. It also helps participants differentiate between what they were taught to believe and what they actually believe.

Materials Needed

Chalkboard or a large sheet of newsprint
Supply of old magazines
Scissors and glue
A medium-size brown paper bag for each participant
Variation 1: A Bible

Procedure

Introduce the activity by saying, "Our own personal images of God may be somewhat different from the image of God conveyed to us by parents, teachers, or preachers. For example, a preacher may talk about an all-loving God, but deep inside ourselves, we may see God as a stern judge. In this activity, we will look at how we see God and then compare these images to the ways others have presented God to us."

Ask the participants to brainstorm the different ways in which teachers, parents, or preachers have talked about God. As the participants call out their ideas, list them on the chalkboard or on a large sheet of newsprint. Do not be afraid to list repeats. Then briefly discuss which images are most common. Before the discussion completely winds down, begin to distribute old magazines, paper bags, scissors, and glue to the participants. Tell the participants to look through the magazines and to cut out three or four pictures that symbolize some characteristics of God that they have heard from teachers, parents, or preachers. Have them glue these pictures on the outside of their paper bags.

Next, have the participants look through the magazines again and cut out three or four pictures that symbolize the characteristics of God that reflect the way they see God in their own lives. These pictures should be placed inside their paper bags.

Then have the participants form groups of four or five. Group members should take turns explaining the meaning of the pictures on the outside of their bags and from whom they learned about these images of God. For example, "This telescope symbolizes that God is always watching me. My mother told me that God sees everything I do."

After everyone has explained his or her choices, the participants should again take turns showing the pictures inside their paper bags and telling how they came to have these particular images of God. For example, a person might show an ad for instant glue and say, "When my life came apart, I felt that God was very, very close to me and that he held me together during a difficult time."

After the members of the small groups have shared their bags, have them discuss these questions:

- Do your inside pictures reflect a different image of God than your outside ones do?
- If they do, what events in your life have caused the inside pictures to be different from the outside ones?
- What insights have you gained from this activity and from listening to one another?

When the participants have finished their discussion, call the groups together, and debrief the participants by asking questions such as these:

- Were there any similarities in your group's paper bags? How were they similar? Why?
- Does this activity reveal any difference between your personal relationship with God and your public sharing of God?
- How can the group help you make your inside pictures better known to other people?

Variations

1. *Images of Jesus.* This activity can be used to have participants find pictures symbolizing characteristics of Jesus.

Read Mark 8:27–30 to the group. Then distribute the same material as suggested above and ask the participants to find pictures that answer the question, "Who do people say I am?" The participants should glue these pictures on the outside of their bags. The participants should then cut out pictures that answer the question, "Who do you say I am?" and put them inside their bags. The same questions listed above should be discussed in the small groups.

2. *Icebreaker.* This activity can also be used as a sharing activity to help participants become better acquainted. On the outside of their bags, have the participants glue pictures that represent how they think other people see them. On the inside of their bags, have them put pictures symbolizing how they see themselves. In the small groups, ask the participants to share why they think there are differences between the way others see them and the way they see themselves.

ACTIVITY 19
Images of the Church

The Church is a mystery that cannot be simply defined. No words can embrace all its aspects or fully express what it is. But by reflecting on the Church's many images and symbols, people can learn to appreciate its complexity and richness. This activity helps participants explore the nature and role of the Church by looking at some of these images and how these images affect their mission as Christians.

Materials Needed

A copy of the Activity Worksheet for each participant
A sheet of drawing paper and a crayon for each participant
Variation 1: Display board, drawing paper, and crayons
Variation 2: Bibles, newsprint, and felt-tip markers

Procedure

Introduce the activity by saying, "All of us have a model, or a concept, of the Church from which we operate. This model shapes how we feel about the Church, what we hope for the Church, and what we expect from the Church. Often, we are not even conscious that this model influences our actions and relationships. But when we sense that other people have a different view of the Church, we may become confused or upset. At times like those, it is good to remember that the other people in the parish are probably operating from a different model. This activity will help us recognize that it is both possible and permissible for people to have different models of the Church and still work together."

Give each participant a copy of the Worksheet, a sheet of drawing paper, and a crayon. Tell the group to put the drawing paper on the side for now. Then read through the Worksheet instructions and answer any questions the participants may have. Remind the group that there are no right or wrong answers. The key words in the instructions are "meaningful to me."

After everyone has finished, ask each participant to look over his or her answers and to pick the image that is most meaningful to him or her. Tell the participants to illustrate their answers on the drawing paper. Mention that since this is not an art class, stick figures are quite acceptable. Then have the participants form small groups, show their illustrations to one another, and share their answers to these questions:

- What comes to mind when you see the image you selected?
- How is this image a symbol of the Church for you?
- What does this image suggest to you about the role of the Church in your life? in the life of others?
- What goes on in your parish that manifests the qualities of this image?

As soon as the discussion groups begin to wind down, call the participants together and debrief them about the activity by discussing the following questions:

- What does the fact that different people have different favorite images of the Church suggest to you?
- How does this fact affect the concept we have that the Church is one?

Variations

1. *Models of the Church.* Parish councils and other committees will find the following variation especially helpful in deciding how best to minister to all people in the parish. Instead of using the images of the Church from the Council document, use the five models presented in Avery Dulles's *Models of the Church* (New York: Doubleday, 1978). Begin by writing the names of the five models on a display board: *servant, institution, herald, community,* and *sacrament.* Brainstorm with the group the meaning of each model. Write the group's ideas next to the appropriate model. Then distribute drawing paper and crayons, and ask each participant to illustrate the model that comes closest to his or her idea of the Church.

   After everyone has finished his or her illustration, have the participants form small groups to share their sketches and to discuss the following questions:

   - Why is each of these models a good image of the Church?

- How do (or don't) these models speak to you about the Church?
- What are the strengths and weaknesses of each model?
- To which groups of people in the parish would each of these models speak most powerfully about the Church? To which groups would they speak least powerfully?

2. *Relating the models of the Church to Scripture.* Have the participants form five groups of no more than seven or eight people each. Give a brief description of Dulles's five models (see Variation 1), and explain that each of these has a basis in Scripture. Then distribute a Bible, a sheet of newsprint, and a felt-tip marker to each group. Assign each group one of the following scriptural passages that echo Dulles's models of the Church: Matthew 25:31–46 (servant), Matthew 16:13–20 (institution), Luke 10:1–16 (herald), 1 Corinthians 12:4–27 (community), and John 15:1–10 (sacrament).

   Have each group answer the following questions, and have one person in each group record the answers on the newsprint.

   - Which of our parish activities reflect this scriptural passage?
   - What kinds of people are attracted to these activities?
   - What are the strengths and weaknesses of this model of the Church?
   - What are the implications of this model of the Church for today?
   - How do you personally relate to this model of the Church?

   Call the five groups together, and ask each group's recorder to describe briefly what was said in the discussion of the questions. After all the groups have shared, debrief the participants about the activity by asking these questions:

   - Why are all of these models of the Church necessary?
   - How does the parish reflect all of these models in what it does?
   - Are there any adjustments the parish might make to reflect a better balance of these models?

101

WORKSHEET
Images of the Church

Below is a list of some images of the Church taken from one of the documents of Vatican II, *The Constitution on the Church in the Modern World*. As you read each image, picture it in your mind and be aware of what kind of response it evokes in you. Then rate each image from 1 to 6. The number 1 means "This image is extremely meaningful to me," and the number 6 means "This image has no meaning for me." The other numbers show shades in between.

1. The vine and the branches

    1   2   3   4   5   6

2. The People of God

    1   2   3   4   5   6

3. The field of God

    1   2   3   4   5   6

4. A tract of land to be cultivated

    1   2   3   4   5   6

5. The Mystical Body

    1   2   3   4   5   6

6. The kingdom

    1   2   3   4   5   6

7. The banquet

    1   2   3   4   5   6

8. The flock

    1   2   3   4   5   6

9. The temple of God

    1   2   3   4   5   6

10. The spouse of the spotless Lamb

    1   2   3   4   5   6

ACTIVITY 20
Creating a Model of the Church

Each person has formed a conscious or unconscious image of the Church which influences his or her relationship to the People of God. This activity engages the participants in a conscious exploration of their own personal images.

Materials Needed

Building blocks
Modeling clay
Construction paper, glue, tape, and scissors
Background music
Variations 1 and 2: Modeling clay

Procedure

Introduce the activity by saying, "Each of us has a personal image of the Church. This image influences not only our expectations of the Church but also the way we live out our membership in the Church. This activity challenges you to describe your personal image of the Church and to share that image with others. There is one catch, however—you may not use words. You are going to express your image by using building blocks, clay, or construction paper. Remember, this activity is not a class on church architecture. Your model should show what you feel the Church is—how the Church functions in your life."

Then invite the participants to file up to the supply table and to select the material with which they want to work. Be sure to tell the participants how much time they have to construct their models. To help get the creative juices flowing, play some appropriate background music while the participants work.

As soon as everyone has completed the assignment, have the participants form groups of four or five and explain their models. To help them with their explanations, have the participants use the questions listed below. Encourage the group members to comment on how each model shows what it means to belong to the Church.

- Why did you create this model of the Church?
- Is this model different from the one with which you grew up? If so, how?
- What does this model show about your expectations of the Church?
- What are you willing to invest of yourself in this model of the Church?

After each person has shared his or her creation, have the group members select the model which they would like to make more operative in their parish. Each group should then present its model to the large group and explain what the model means and why it was selected.

Debrief the participants about the activity by discussing the following questions:

- What model of the Church is predominant in this group?
- What is the predominant model of the Church at work in our parish?
- In what way does the parish manifest all of these models?
- What are the practical implications of the fact that different people have different models of the Church?

Variations

1. *Working in small groups.* Skip the individual models, and have the participants immediately form small groups. Each group should first discuss what its members expect from the parish and the Church, and then decide on how to express those expectations with modeling clay. After the groups have created their models, they should take turns presenting them to the large group. Discuss the experience with the participants by using the debriefing questions listed above.

2. *Changing images.* Give the participants some modeling clay, and ask them each to make two models of the Church. These models should reflect how they experienced or felt about the Church during two different periods in their lives. When the participants have completed their work, have them gather in small groups to share their models and to discuss the following questions:

- How did you feel about the Church at the times depicted?
- What did you once believe about the Church that you no longer believe?
- What events or persons caused the change?
- In what way do you feel you are now better or worse off than you once were?
- How is your view of the Church changing at the present time?

ACTIVITY 21
Picture Study

Human beings are not merely transmitters of what they see and hear. It is almost impossible for people to tell the facts and only the facts. Inevitably, they will color, or interpret, the facts based on their insights, feelings, and experiences. This activity provides the participants with an opportunity not only to focus on the facts but also to explore what their interpretations tell about their lives.

Materials Needed

Copies of a photograph or a picture from a magazine
A sheet of paper and a pencil for each participant
Variation 2: Bibles

Procedure

Introduce the activity by saying, "Most of us make good use of the left side of the brain, which controls the logical reasoning powers. But we seldom use the right side of the brain, which controls the imagination and the creative part of our personalities. This activity challenges us to use our imaginations. First, each of us is going to study a picture. Then, we will try to discover what our reactions to the picture tell about our feelings and our lives."

Invite the participants to form groups of four or five, and pass out a sheet of paper and a pencil to each participant. Then give each group a copy of the same photograph or magazine picture. (The picture you select for this activity should be very sharp and show a lot of detail. Some examples are a picture of a garden, a tree, an old house, or a crowded shopping mall.) Explain to the participants that the activity has three steps and that they are going to complete these steps one at a time.

Step 1. Have the participants study the picture closely for a few minutes and then list as accurately as possible all the details they can see in the picture. They should not try to explain or to interpret the details or the picture. After the participants have completed their lists, have them share with the other members of their group all the details they observed.

Step 2. Tell the participants that each person who studies the picture will find a slightly different meaning in it. Have the participants study the picture again and write down what it says to them. Then have the participants share their responses in the small groups.

Step 3. Ask the participants to look at the picture for a third time and then write down what they have learned about themselves by studying the picture. When everyone has finished, have the participants share their responses in the small groups.

After a reasonable amount of time, call the groups together and debrief the participants about the activity by asking the following:

- How difficult did you find this activity?
- What feelings did this activity surface in you?

Variations

1. *Observing as a group.* Instead of having each person write down his or her own observations about the picture, have the groups look at the picture and work together to list the details. Members of each group should then take turns telling what the picture means to them and what they have learned about themselves.

2. *Relating the activity to Scripture.* At the conclusion of the activity, have each participant tell about a Scripture story he or she feels pertains to the meaning of the picture. Have on hand several Bibles for those who need them.

3. *Reflecting on group relationships.* This same activity can be used to reflect on what the picture says about a particular group—the family, the school, a club. The first and second steps remain the same. In the third step, however, ask the participants to share what the picture says about the group and what they have learned about their relationships in the group.

ACTIVITY 22
Pictures of Jesus

There are many different images of Jesus. Each of these images reflects a particular role or quality of Jesus; for example, Jesus the Teacher, Jesus the Good Shepherd, Jesus the Risen Lord. This activity helps participants become more aware of their own "pictures" of Jesus and how these pictures affect their growth as Christians.

Materials Needed

Several depictions of Jesus—a significant variety
Variation 1: Drawing paper and crayons or markers
Variation 3: Newsprint and a marker
Variation 4: Old magazines and scissors

Procedure

Introduce the activity by saying, "All of us have our own mental images of what Jesus looked like. Whenever we hear his name, those images come to mind. While our images may change with the context, one image will usually be favored over others. Along with this image, we also have an image of Jesus with which we do not 'resonate'—one we do not like. During this activity, we are going to look at some pictures of Jesus to see which of them comes closest to our predominant image of him. After that, we will pick the one that is least like our image of Jesus."

Spread the pictures of Jesus out on a table. (The pictures you select should include old images and contemporary ones, simple and complicated ones, as well as Jesus in his various roles.) Ask the participants to gather around the table and to look at the pictures. Each participant should mentally choose two pictures—the one closest to his or her image of Jesus and the one least like his or her image of Jesus. After everyone has chosen two pictures, have the participants form groups of three or four and discuss their choices.

When the discussions wind down, call the groups together, and debrief the participants about the activity with these questions:

- What did you learn from this experience?
- During the liturgical year, the Church presents various images of Jesus. What are the images suggested by Christmas? Holy Week? Easter? Pentecost? Ordinary Time?
- What aspects or qualities of our Lord does each of these images emphasize?
- Why is it helpful to have so many different images of Jesus?
- How do your personal needs influence which image of Jesus is predominant in your mind?

Variations

1. *Titles of Jesus.* Instead of showing pictures to the group, name the various titles of Jesus (for example, Lord, Son of David, Son of Man, Savior, Emmanuel, Teacher), and ask the participants to draw pictures that show how they feel about each title and to explain why they feel that way.
2. *Liturgical seasons.* During one of the liturgical seasons, display a picture showing the role of Jesus celebrated during that season. Ask the participants to discuss the following questions:

   - How do you feel when you see this picture of Jesus?
   - How could this image affect the way you pray or act?
   - Do you have any negative reactions to this image of Jesus? Why?
   - What does this image of Jesus say to you about your life at the present time?
   - Why do you think the Church presents so many different images of Jesus to us during the liturgical year?

3. *The life cycle.* On a large sheet of newsprint, list the seven stages a person travels through during his or her lifetime: infancy, childhood, adolescence, young adulthood, midlife, older adulthood, old age. Then discuss the following questions with the group:

   - What are some of the needs people have during each of these stages?
   - Which image of Jesus most responds to the needs of people in each stage? Why?

- What does this activity tell you about sharing? about the way people see Jesus?
- What does this activity tell you about your relationship to Jesus?
- What image of Jesus best responds to your present situation?

4. *Other images of Jesus.* Ask the group to look through old magazines, and have each participant cut out four pictures that tell him or her something about Jesus. Then have the participants form small groups and take turns sharing why these pictures speak to them about Jesus. Afterward, debrief the participants about the activity by discussing these questions:

- What did you learn from this activity?
- Why is it important to be open to other people's images of Jesus?

4

Storytelling

Storytelling is the oldest and perhaps the most effective way for people to share their experiences and to express their identity. But storytelling involves more than a mere recitation of facts. It involves people's feelings and interpretation of the events in their stories. It also helps people understand the past, take control of the present, and plan for the future.

People have unique stories to tell not only about their relationships with God and with others but about the positive and negative influences in their lives. By telling their stories to others, people are able to share their faith journeys. Conversely, listening to the stories of others helps them gain new insights into life. Finally, by connecting their lives with Scripture stories, people can gain a clearer understanding of the New Testament.

WHAT TO EXPECT

Through these activities the participants will learn to accept and to own their life stories and experiences. In other words, they will appreciate their life's journey as uniquely their own. The sharing of stories helps them see the power of God at work, helps them evaluate what is going on in their lives, and helps them plan how they wish to live. The activities also help the participants see the relationship between various events in their lives and provide them with a safe and comfortable way to share their experiences of Jesus. While the discussion of ideas sometimes divides people, sharing stories can develop a common bond and a strong sense of solidarity among people. When people realize that others have gone through the same kinds of experiences that they have had, they feel a kinship with them. As a result of sharing their stories, people can see themselves and their lives in the light of Jesus.

- Activity 23, "Sharing Scripture Stories," helps the participants grow in their relationships with Jesus and others.
- Activity 24, "The Call to Ministry," helps the participants recognize how the Lord is calling them to ministry.
- Activity 25, "Qualities of Discipleship," shows the participants how the New Testament descriptions of discipleship apply to their own lives.
- Activity 26, "Theological Reflection," helps the participants look at their everyday lives to see how the power of God is at work.
- Activity 27, "The Synoptic Gospels," outlines for the participants the social and religious context in which the synoptic Gospels were written.

INTENDED AUDIENCE

The activities in this chapter work well with groups of all ages. They are especially helpful if the participants do not know one another, because they offer a comfortable yet meaningful introduction. For example, telling a favorite Scripture story enables teenagers, who are usually shy about discussing their religious experiences, to share their faith and understanding of Jesus.

These activities are especially effective on retreats or during any extended period of time that people spend together to deepen their relationship with Jesus. They also work well with groups of people who are confused about how to relate to Jesus and how to grow in that relationship.

ACTIVITY 23
Sharing Scripture Stories

Much of Scripture is in narrative form. The narratives of Scripture convey more than a sequence of events. They also convey the feelings and insights of the storytellers. When people retell stories from the Scriptures in their own words, they color these stories with their own feelings and insights.

Materials Needed

A Bible (or a New Testament) for each participant
Candles—one for each small group
A sheet of newsprint and a felt-tip marker for each small
   group
Tape

Procedure

Introduce the activity by saying, "The Scriptures basically are stories—stories that reveal God's love for people and their efforts to respond to this love. By reading these stories, we can learn much about who we are and how we can grow in our response to God's love. This learning and growth come when we recognize the psychological process at work in these stories, identify the truths buried in them, and see the relationship of Scripture to our lives. In this activity, we are going to share our faith by telling our favorite stories about Jesus. In doing so, we can get in touch with our own stages of religious development, share our insights into the faith, and become more aware of the changes that have taken place in our relationship to God."

Explain to the participants that there are four steps in the activity and that you will describe each step as the group moves along.

Step 1. Be sure that everyone has a Bible. Then tell the participants to page through the New Testament and find a favorite story about Jesus. After they have made their selections, they should spend some time reading and reflecting on their stories. (Note: Be available to help those who have difficulty in selecting an appropriate story.)

Give the participants at least five minutes to meditate, and then have them form small groups. When everyone is comfortable, place a lighted candle in the middle of each group and dim the room lights.

Instruct the groups that each participant should tell his or her story about Jesus and briefly explain why the story is his or her favorite. Emphasize that the participants should tell the stories in their own words, not read them. Make sure group members understand that they are not to correct the way a person interprets a story, nor should they try to offer a different interpretation of the story. They are merely supposed to listen.

Step 2. When all the participants have shared their stories, give each group a sheet of newsprint and a marker. Have each group member express his or her favorite attitude or characteristic of Jesus as found in the story he or she told. One person in the group should record these answers on the newsprint.

Step 3. Call all the groups together. Ask the recorder from each group to tape the newsprint to the wall where everyone can see it and to read the list of traits, identifying the stories from which they were derived.

Step 4. Bring the activity to a close in one of the following ways: (a) Use the material taped on the wall to lead into a discussion about Jesus or the Scriptures. (b) Have each participant select another story about Jesus that he or she feels is especially relevant at this particular time in his or her life and share the story with the group. (c) Have the participants return to their small groups, and ask them to pick one of Jesus' attitudes or characteristics that they feel they have in common. Each group member should then describe an incident that manifested this attitude or characteristic in his or her life. (d) Have the participants identify some of their favorite stories about Jesus from the past and state why they now have different favorite stories. This will help participants see how they have changed and perhaps grown in their relationship with Jesus.

Variations

1. *Parish councils.* Sharing favorite stories about Jesus can be especially effective in parish council meetings. If the council is having a particularly difficult time with some

matter, the council members can postpone the discussion for a few minutes and reflect on which story from the New Testament seems to throw some light on the situation. Then each person can share a story and tell why he or she thinks it contributes to the discussion.

If the parish council is trying to set goals or make a needs assessment of the parish, each person might select a story from the New Testament that he or she thinks the parish needs to hear at this time. After everyone has shared his or her story, the council can compile a list of the attitudes of Jesus drawn from these stories and discuss how these attitudes are manifested in the parish. The council can then determine what needs to be done to increase these attitudes in the parish community.

2. *Favorite people stories.* Instead of having participants share a favorite story about Jesus, ask them to relate their favorite story about a parent, a spouse, a close friend, or some person the entire group knows. After sharing a story, each participant should describe the human qualities of the person and explain how the incident related has affected his or her life.

3. *Funeral services.* This activity can be very helpful and comforting in planning a funeral. By listening to the members of the family share their favorite stories about the deceased and tell how the deceased affected their lives, the priest or other liturgical minister is able to establish the proper tone for the funeral service. Hearing these stories also enables the priest to be more personal in his homily. The stories could be recorded on tape as they are being told, or they could be written down at a later time as a permanent record to help the family members keep alive their memories of the deceased.

ACTIVITY 24
The Call to Ministry

This activity presents the call of the disciples and engages the group in an imaginary participation in this story. By entering into this story, participants discover how the Lord is calling them to service and how they can respond.

Materials Needed

A Bible
A sheet of paper and a pencil for each participant
A copy of the Activity Worksheet for each participant

Procedure

Introduce the activity by saying, "The call to ministry usually comes to us in a very ordinary way. Something happens and we realize that the Lord has called us. I am going to read the story of the call of the first Apostles. As you listen to the story, think of yourself as one of the Apostles who was fishing. Imagine that you are either Peter, Andrew, John, or James. Put yourself into the scene. Feel, hear, see, and smell what is going on. After I finish the reading, I will pause for a moment to allow the scene to come alive on the screen of your imagination."

Slowly and dramatically read Matthew 4:18–22. When you finish, pause for a few moments, and then ask the participants to jot down on a piece of paper which Apostle they imagined themselves to be. Tell them, "Describe what you *saw*: for example, what the people looked like, the kind of boat you saw, what the lake looked like, what the people were doing." When the participants have finished writing, ask them to describe what they *heard* various people saying: Jesus, the other fishermen, the people standing on the shore, the father of James and John. Allow enough time for writing and then ask the participants to describe two things they *felt*: for example, heat, cold, wind, earth. Finally, have the participants describe what they *smelled* at the scene: for example, the smell of the fish, the fire, the wind blowing off the lake.

After everyone has finished writing, have the participants

gather into groups of four or five and share their impressions of what they, as Apostles, saw, heard, felt, and smelled.

Next, pass out copies of the Worksheet and have each participant circle the answer in each group that is closest to his or her reaction to the scene. Afterward, have the participants share their answers in their small groups and give their reasons for their answers.

Call the groups together and debrief the participants about the activity by discussing the following questions:

- How do you think the call of the Lord usually comes to people?
- Are there any signs in your life that show the Lord is calling you?
- What do you think the Lord is calling you to do?
- How do you feel about this call?

WORKSHEET
The Call to Ministry

You have imagined yourself being called by Jesus along with the other Apostles. Below are some possible responses to this call. Circle the one response which is closest to your own feelings.

1. I am one of the four people in the boat and I hear Jesus calling me. My first reaction is

   a. Does he mean me?
   b. What does he mean, "fishers of men"?
   c. That man on the beach must be a little crazy!
   d. Wow! This is a chance to make it big!
   e. I can't go! I've got to think of my family.

2. My first impression of Jesus is

   a. Who is this man wandering along the beach?
   b. This fellow must be desperate for a following if he's calling me.
   c. This man has something I want, but I'm not sure what it is.
   d. This man looks like an enterprising type. He's going places, and I'm going with him.
   e. He is the Messiah, the one we are looking for.

3. I decide to follow Jesus because

   a. I have heard about him from others and am intrigued about what they said about him. I want to find out more.
   b. Fishing is boring. I want a change.
   c. My life needs a spiritual uplift. This is just what I need.
   d. The others are going. I don't want to be left behind.
   e. He is so powerful that I have to follow him.

4. I am sitting near the beach and watching the whole scene. I think

   a. Those guys are nuts to go with him.
   b. Damn! I'm always in the wrong place. I wasn't invited.
   c. Now I suppose they are going to be rabble-rousers, too.

d. That man sure is powerful. I'm glad he didn't call me.

e. They are doing the right thing. You have to take chances in life.

5. A few years have passed since I first answered the call to follow Jesus. Now

a. I wonder how I got into this situation.

b. I wonder who is looking after my family and business.

c. I think I did a foolish thing by leaving so suddenly.

d. I believe Jesus is so great that everyone should understand why I ran after him.

e. I wonder what is in store for me in the future.

6. If Jesus were to walk up to me right now and say, "Drop everything and come follow me," I would respond

a. Wait until I talk it over with my family and friends. I'll give you my answer in a few days.

b. Yes, Lord. I'm ready to go.

c. I'll be right there. Just let me pick up some clothes and a few other things I might need on the journey.

d. You must be kidding. What's your angle?

e. Not right now. I'll come as soon as I finish up some important business.

ACTIVITY 25
Qualities of Discipleship

Nowhere in the Gospels does Jesus give a job description for a disciple. But throughout the Gospels, there are stories and teachings which give some insight into discipleship. This activity helps the participants explore discipleship in the Gospels.

Materials Needed

A Bible for each participant
A sheet of newsprint and a felt-tipped marker for each small
  group
Chalkboard or display board
A sheet of paper and a pencil for each participant
Variation 2: Old magazines, poster board, scissors, and glue
Variation 4: Drawing paper and finger paints

Procedure

Introduce the activity by saying, "Scattered throughout the Gospels are stories that describe the qualities of those who wish to be followers of Jesus. In this activity, we are going to look at some of these stories and draw a composite picture of what is expected from a disciple of Jesus. We are also going to see how this composite picture relates to our own lives as Christians."

Be sure that every participant has a Bible. Then direct the participants to form small groups of seven people and to select a group reporter. Give each reporter a sheet of newsprint and a marker, and have him or her write the following column headings at the top of the newsprint: *Gospel Passage* and *Quality.* Under the first heading, have the reporter list the following passages: *Mark 1:14–20, Mark 6:7–13, Mark 10:35–45, Luke 9:23–25, Luke 10:25–37, Luke 12:22–31,* and *Luke 12:35–40.* Then go around to each group and assign one of the passages to each participant. Instruct the participants to read their stories silently and to be prepared (1) to retell the stories in their own words and (2) to identify the qualities of discipleship highlighted in the stories. Give the participants eight to ten minutes to complete the assignment.

When time is up, have each participant tell his or her story to the others in the group and identify the quality of discipleship that is reflected in the story. After each presentation, the group reporter should record on the newsprint the quality of discipleship suggested by the participant.

When all the groups have finished, have the reporter from each group share with the whole group the qualities listed on the newsprint. The reporter should present only those qualities that previous groups have not mentioned. As the groups share their lists, write each quality on the chalkboard or on a display board. In the end, if you have listed more than seven qualities, have the participants select seven of the items by voting on each one with a show of hands. Keep only the seven items with the most votes. Then distribute paper and pencils, and have each participant write down the seven qualities that the group has selected. Tell the participants to rate themselves on how operative these qualities are in their lives, using a scale of 1 to 5. 1 means "highly operative," and 5 means "not very operative."

After everyone has finished writing, have the participants share in their small groups the two qualities that are most operative in their lives and give examples of how these qualities are manifested.

When the discussions begin to wind down, call the participants together and debrief them about the activity by discussing the following questions:

- What did you learn about yourself from this activity?
- In which areas do you need to grow as a disciple of Christ?

Variations

1. Group assessment. Instead of having participants assess themselves as individuals, ask them to rate themselves as a group on each of the seven qualities. Then discuss how the group manifests the two highest rated qualities and what it might do to improve in the areas the group rated itself low.

2. *Creating collages.* Ask each group to look through old magazines for pictures that illustrate the seven qualities that were selected and to make a collage. Afterward, have each group show its collage and explain why the particular pictures were chosen.
3. *Role-playing.* Ask each small group to create and mime a skit that would show one of the seven qualities in action in daily life.
4. *Finger painting.* Give each participant a large sheet of drawing paper and some finger paints. Tell the participants to create a painting (abstract or realistic) that demonstrates one quality of discipleship. Then hang the paintings around the room for all to view.

ACTIVITY 26
Theological Reflection

The adult Christian is one who can see the relationship between faith and life, and who can act on this knowledge. The process a person uses to relate faith to life is called theological reflection. There are many ways to go through a theological reflection. This activity represents one such way. Moreover, it is an exercise which can make a person more comfortable with the process.

Materials Needed

A copy of the Activity Worksheet for each participant
Pencils

Procedure

Introduce the activity by saying, "Not many of us consider ourselves theologians. Being a theologian sounds like something for saints or university professors. But every adult Christian needs to be a theologian in the strict sense of the term—a believer who is seeking understanding. The exercise you are about to do will help you as a believer see the relationship between what you believe and what you are experiencing in your life."

Distribute copies of the Worksheet and quickly review the directions. If you think it would be helpful, go through each of the steps on the Worksheet using an example from your own life. Answer any questions the participants may have, and then have them begin their Worksheets. Tell the group that everyone has five minutes to complete this part of the activity.

When time is up, collect everyone's pencil, and have the participants form groups of four. Explain that each person has ten minutes to share his or her Worksheet. The other group members are not to correct or add, but they may ask questions that will help clarify the information. If there is time, they may also relate similar incidents from their own lives and explain what insights they gained from them. To make sure that everyone has a chance to share, mark off each ten-minute interval by calling out, "Next person."

When the groups have finished, debrief the participants about the activity by discussing the following questions:

- What did you learn from this activity?
- How can you use this activity in your daily life?

WORKSHEET
Theological Reflection

There are four steps in this theological reflection. For each step, read the short introduction and then answer the questions by jotting down two or three key words. These words will help you share your reflection with the group.

1. *Step 1: Data.* Think of an experience that had special meaning for you and that had some implications for your life. It can be a personal experience or something you read about in the news which affected you.

   a. What happened?

   b. Who was involved?

   c. When and where did it happen?

   d. What were the effects or consequences of the experience?

2. *Step 2: Analysis.* Set the experience in the broader context of your life.

   a. How did you feel about the experience?

b. What factors in your background contributed to the experience, for example, family, ethnic origin, education?

c. Which of your attitudes and values influenced the experience?

d. What was the key issue in the experience?

e. What pattern of acting was evident?

3. *Step 3: Meaning.* Explore the scriptural and theological implications of the experience to see how the event influenced your relationship to God.

a. How was the hand of God evident in the experience?

b. What Scripture stories seem relevant to the experience?

c. What theological category seems to fit the experience, for example, grace, original sin, forgiveness, redemption, providence?

d. How can theology help you attach meaning to the experience?

4. *Step 4: Action.* Reflection is not enough; you need to act on your new insights.

a. What have you learned by this reflection?

b. What one specific action are you going to take as a result of what you have learned?

ACTIVITY 27
The Synoptic Gospels

Long before the Gospels were written, the words and actions of Jesus were preached orally. The final written Gospels were the products of different faith communities. By introducing the participants to the synoptic Gospels, this activity will show how each evangelist chose certain stories to record and others to eliminate based on the needs of the community.

Materials Needed

Copies of Activity Worksheets A–F for each small group
Writing paper, a large sheet of newsprint, and a felt-tipped
    pen for each small group
Several pairs of scissors and tape
A copy of Activity Worksheet G for each participant
Variation: Several Bibles for reference

Procedure

Introduce the activity by reading aloud John 20:30–31: "Jesus performed many other signs as well—signs not recorded here—in the presence of his disciples. But these have been recorded to help you believe that Jesus is the Messiah, the Son of God, so that through this faith you may have life in his name."

Then give this explanation: "The passage I just read from the Gospel according to John suggests that the early preachers and writers considered some of the teachings and actions of Jesus more important than others. They realized that some would have a more direct bearing on the lives of the people to whom they were preaching or for whom they were writing and so would help their audiences see more clearly that Jesus was the Messiah. Nowhere is this more evident than in the Gospels according to Matthew, Mark, and Luke. These three versions of the Good News are called synoptic Gospels because they are alike in structure, and their similarities and differences can be seen at a glance. The writers and preachers of these books picked material that would be most helpful in their efforts to spread the Good News. For example, the stories of the Prodigal Son, the Good Samaritan, and the Good Thief are found only in the Gospel according to Luke. We may well ask why such powerful and important stories are not found in Matthew or Mark. The obvious answer is that Luke must have felt that the community for which he was writing had a special need to hear about the mercy and compassion of God. In this activity, we are going to try to capture the process by which the synoptic Gospels were formed."

Have the participants form groups of six. Pass out copies of Worksheets A–F to each group, giving a different Worksheet to each person. Then explain to the groups: "Imagine that the six of you are living somewhere in the Near East about the year A.D. 70. You are deeply committed Christians, and you want to put together a written account of the deeds and sayings of Jesus. Thirty or forty years have passed since the death of Jesus, and you feel it is imperative that you write down the most important stories about him so that they will not be lost to the next generation. You want these stories to be relevant to your children, to lead them to a deeper faith in Jesus as the Son of God, the Messiah. Now, read the directions on your Worksheet. You have about ten minutes to complete this part of the activity."

When the participants have finished their Worksheets, tell the groups that they have about twenty-five minutes for members to tell their stories and to share their answers to the questions. Remind the participants that they should tell the stories in their own words, not read them.

As soon as time is up, stop the discussions, and distribute writing paper, a sheet of newsprint, and a felt-tipped pen to each group. Explain that in the next step of the activity, the groups should pretend to be evangelists. Their task is to decide on the order in which the six stories should be recorded so that they can help future Christians know and follow Jesus. Each group should discuss the order, and the order should be arrived at by mutual agreement. A recording secretary should keep track of the discussion in order to prepare a summary of the rationale the group had for its order.

When the groups have established the order of the stories, direct the participants to "proclaim" their Gospels by cutting out the stories and taping them in order on the sheet of newsprint. Each group should give its Gospel a title. In addition, have the secretary write a summary of the group's rationale at the bottom of the newsprint.

After all the groups are finished, display the work. Let each group present its Gospel. Then have a group discussion of what has happened. When the discussion dies down, point out that this exercise has shown in miniature how the synoptic Gospels came to be written.

Finally, distribute copies of Worksheet G and briefly go over the instructions. To help the participants get started on their project, point out that Matthew wrote primarily for Jewish Christians and wanted to show that Jesus was the expected Messiah—the king of Israel. Mark wrote for the Gentile Christians and emphasized Jesus' humanity and role as Savior. Luke's audience, on the other hand, was Greek and poor, so he stressed Jesus' healing, compassion, and mercy.

Variation

Creative evangelists. Do the activity as described but give the participants the opportunity to substitute one or two other Gospel stories for the ones on the Worksheets. They should, however, have a total of six, so they will have to eliminate a story for each one they add. Urge the groups to go through the same process with the new stories as was used on the Worksheets.

WORKSHEET A
The Synoptic Gospels

Below is a story about Jesus that has been circulating in your faith community. It is a story that you yourself have heard and told many times. After reflecting on the story, answer the questions. Be ready to share the story in your own words.

The Great Commandment

One of the scribes came up to Jesus and asked him, "Which is the first of all the commandments?" Jesus replied: "This is the first:

'Hear, O Israel! The Lord our God is Lord alone!
Therefore you shall love the Lord your God
with all your heart,
with all your soul,
with all your mind,
and with all your strength.'
This is the second,
'You shall love your neighbor as yourself.'

There is no other commandment greater than these." The scribe said to him: "Excellent, Teacher! You are right in saying, 'He is the One, there is no other than he.' Yes, 'to love him with all our heart, with all our thoughts and with all our strength, and to love our neighbor as ourselves' is worth more than any burnt offering or sacrifice." Jesus approved the insight of this answer and told him, "You are not far from the reign of God." And no one had the courage to ask him any more questions.

1. Why has this story been preserved in our community?

2. What does this story tell about Jesus and his activity in today's world?

3. Why should this story continue to be preserved?

WORKSHEET B
The Synoptic Gospels

Below is a story about Jesus that has been circulating in your faith community. It is a story that you yourself have heard and told many times. After reflecting on the story, answer the questions. Be ready to share the story in your own words.

The Healing of a Leper

A leper approached Jesus with a request, kneeling down as he addressed him: "If you will to do so, you can cure me." Moved with pity, Jesus stretched out his hand, touched him, and said: "I do will it. Be cured." The leprosy left him then and there, and he was cured. Jesus gave him a stern warning and sent him on his way. "Not a word to anyone, now," he said. "Go off and present yourself to the priest and offer for your cure what Moses prescribed. That should be proof for them." The man went off and began to proclaim the whole matter freely, making the story public. As a result of this, it was no longer possible for Jesus to enter a town openly. He stayed in desert places; yet people kept coming to him from all sides.

1. Why has this story been preserved in our community?

2. What does this story tell about Jesus and his activity in today's world?

3. Why should this story continue to be preserved?

WORKSHEET C
The Synoptic Gospels

Below is a story about Jesus that has been circulating in your faith community. It is a story that you yourself have heard and told many times. After reflecting on the story, answer the questions. Be ready to share the story in your own words.

Peter's Profession of Faith

Then Jesus and his disciples set out for the villages around Caesarea Philippi. On the way he asked his disciples this question: "Who do people say that I am?" They replied, "Some, John the Baptizer, others, Elijah, still others, one of the prophets." "And you," he went on to ask, "who do you say that I am?" Peter answered him, "You are the Messiah!" Then he gave them strict orders not to tell anyone about him.

He began to teach them that the Son of Man had to suffer much, be rejected by the elders, the chief priests, and the scribes, be put to death, and rise three days later. He said these things quite openly. Peter then took him aside and began to remonstrate with him. At this he turned around and, eyeing the disciples, reprimanded Peter: "Get out of my sight, you Satan! You are not judging by God's standards but by man's!"

1. Why has this story been preserved in our community?

2. What does this story tell about Jesus and his activity in today's world?

3. Why should this story continue to be preserved?

WORKSHEET D
The Synoptic Gospels

Below is a story about Jesus that has been circulating in your faith community. It is a story that you yourself have heard and told many times. After reflecting on the story, answer the questions. Be ready to share the story in your own words.

The Healing of a Blind Man

They came to Jericho next, and as Jesus was leaving that place with his disciples and a sizable crowd, there was a blind beggar Bartimaeus sitting by the roadside. On hearing that it was Jesus of Nazareth, he began to call out, "Jesus, Son of David, have pity on me!" Many people were scolding him to make him keep quiet, but he shouted all the louder, "Son of David, have pity on me!" Then Jesus stopped and said, "Call him over." So they called the blind man over, telling him as they did so, "You have nothing to fear from him! Get up! He is calling you!" He threw aside his cloak, jumped up and came to Jesus. Jesus asked him, "What do you want me to do for you?" "Rabboni," the blind man said, "I want to see." Jesus said in reply, "Be on your way! Your faith has healed you." Immediately he received his sight and started to follow him up the road.

1. Why has this story been preserved in our community?

2. What does this story tell about Jesus and his activity in today's world?

3. Why should this story continue to be preserved?

WORKSHEET E
The Synoptic Gospels

Below is a story about Jesus that has been circulating in your faith community. It is a story that you yourself have heard and told many times. After reflecting on the story, answer the questions. Be ready to share the story in your own words.

The Parable of the Mustard Seed

Jesus went on to say: "What comparison shall we use for the reign of God? What image will help to present it? It is like a mustard seed which, when planted in the soil, is the smallest of all the earth's seeds, yet once it is sown, springs up to become the largest of shrubs, with branches big enough for the birds of the sky to build nests in its shade."

1. Why has this story been preserved in our community?

2. What does this story tell about Jesus and his activity in today's world?

3. Why should this story continue to be preserved?

WORKSHEET F
The Synoptic Gospels

Below is a story about Jesus that has been circulating in your faith community. It is a story that you yourself have heard and told many times. After reflecting on the story, answer the questions. Be ready to share the story in your own words.

The Feeding of the Five Thousand

Upon disembarking Jesus saw a vast crowd. He pitied them, for they were like sheep without a shepherd; and he began to teach them at great length. It was now getting late and his disciples came to him with a suggestion: "This is a deserted place and it is already late. Why do you not dismiss them so that they can go to the crossroads and villages around here and buy themselves something to eat?" "You give them something to eat," Jesus replied. At that they said, "Are we to go and spend two hundred days' wages for bread to feed them?" "How many loaves have you?" Jesus asked. "Go and see." When they learned the number they answered, "Five, and two fish." He told them to make the people sit down on the green grass in groups or parties. The people took their places in hundreds and fifties, neatly arranged like flower beds. Then, taking the five loaves and the two fish, Jesus raised his eyes to heaven, pronounced a blessing, broke the loaves, and gave them to the disciples to distribute. He divided the two fish among all of them and they ate until they had their fill. They gathered up enough leftovers to fill twelve baskets.

1. Why has this story been preserved in our community?

2. What does this story tell about Jesus and his activity in today's world?

3. Why should this story continue to be preserved?

WORKSHEET G
The Synoptic Gospels

Now that you have some understanding of how the synoptic Gospels were written, it can be very interesting to review how the stories you studied are actually used by Matthew, Mark, and Luke. During the next week, use this sheet as a tour of the synoptics. Follow each story through the three Gospels. Study the similarities and differences. Draw your own conclusions as to the rationale each Gospel writer had in telling each story. Record your thoughts on the reverse side of the page.

1. The Healing of a Leper

   Matthew 8:1–4
   Mark 1:40–45
   Luke 5:12–16

2. The Parable of the Mustard Seed

   Matthew 3:31–32
   Mark 4:30–32
   Luke 13:18–19

3. The Feeding of the Five Thousand

   Matthew 14:13–21
   Mark 6:34–44
   Luke 9:10–17

4. Peters Profession of Faith

   Matthew 16:13–23
   Mark 8:27–33
   Luke 9:18–22

5. The Healing of a Blind Man

   Matthew 20:29–34
   Mark 10:46–52
   Luke 18:35–43

6. The Great Commandment

   Matthew 22:34–40
   Mark 12:28–31
   Luke 10:25–27

5

Role-Playing

Role-playing is a very exciting, action-oriented way of getting in touch with oneself and with the experiences of others. This meeting with self and others allows the participants the opportunity to reexperience past events as though they were occurring at the present time. As the participants play roles or observe roles being played, they can see and feel the world through a new pair of eyes and a new set of feelings.

In these activities, participants are asked to play various roles based on Scripture and on past events in their lives. Role-playing and dialoging with the people in Scripture are excellent ways to learn about and appreciate the Bible. These same techniques may be used with people or events from a person's past to help him or her understand better what actually occurred and how he or she reacted.

WHAT TO EXPECT

Role-playing provides a different way of looking at and evaluating life. By playing roles and observing others play roles and by sharing their feelings with the group, participants learn how others feel and think. They see that there may be many valid responses to any given situation or problem. This process gives them the opportunity to gain new insights into self, others, and the Scriptures, and from these new insights come a broader understanding and acceptance of reality so that new ways of relating to people and of doing things can be discovered.

Because role-playing activities engage all of a person's faculties and attention, new things are revealed in a different

139

light. Role-playing requires a high degree of participation and therefore generates a great deal of discussion.

Role-playing is an enjoyable way to build community. A bond is created among the participants as they grow in trust and as they share deeply about their lives.

- Activity 28, "The Spiritual Journey of Peter," helps the participants see their own struggles to follow Jesus in Peter's struggles.
- Activity 29, "Role-Playing the Christmas Story," sheds light on the person of Jesus, using the Gospels according to Matthew and Luke.
- Activity 30, "Interviewing Biblical Characters," reveals the meaning of New Testament stories by showing their impact on the people involved in them.
- Activity 31, "Dialoging with a Parable," lets the participants use their imaginations to get in touch with the various elements in a parable.
- Activity 32, "Eyewitness," has the participants role-play the passion narrative in order to have it shape and give direction to their lives.
- Activity 33, "Role-Playing the Past," helps the participants look at the past in a positive manner and see how it influences the present.

INTENDED AUDIENCE

The activities in this chapter can be used with a wide variety of groups and with all ages. They work especially well with groups who wish to grow in their understanding of themselves, of others, and of Scripture. The activities are especially useful if a group tends to be nonverbal and needs variety in the learning experience. Young people enjoy this technique and easily share their thoughts and feelings when playing roles. Adults who enjoy sharing and adventure will also like these activities and will find them an interesting alternative to other types of learning such as lectures and retreats.

ACTIVITY 28
The Spiritual Journey of Peter

The Apostle Peter often struggled with his faith in Jesus. By role-playing incidents in the life of Peter, the participants gain a deeper appreciation of their own journeys of faith and the struggles they encounter along the way.

Materials Needed

A Bible for each participant
Chalkboard or a display board
Variation: A sheet of newsprint and a felt-tipped marker for
   each group

Procedure

Introduce the activity by explaining the benefits of role-playing. The introduction to the chapter will help you do this. Then tell the participants they are going to have the chance to role-play the Apostle Peter. This does not mean that they have to be impressive speakers or great actors. All they have to do is get in touch with how Peter might have felt or what he might have thought during certain events in his life. By entering into Peter's struggle to follow the Lord, the participants can learn more about themselves and their own efforts to follow Jesus.

Be sure that everyone has a Bible, and then ask the participants to form groups of seven. As the participants are getting settled, write the following list on the chalkboard or on a display board:

1. The call of Peter—Matthew 4:18–22
2. Peter's response—Luke 5:1–11
3. Jesus walks on the water—Matthew 14:22–33
4. Peter the Rock—Matthew 16:13–20
5. Peter's denial—Matthew 26:69–75
6. Peter the Shepherd—John 21:1–23
7. The cure of a cripple—Acts 3:1–10

Assign each group member a different passage from the list. Then explain that each participant should carefully read the passage and prepare to tell the story to the group. The story must be told in the first person. Along with describing the sequence of events, the participant should include the following three aspects in his or her presentation: (1) the physical—what Peter experienced through his senses, (2) the emotional—what Peter felt, and (3) the spiritual—what impact the story's events had on Peter's life.

To help the participants get in the spirit of the activity, you may want to share the following examples. They are based on Matthew's story of the transfiguration (see 17:1–8).

- *The physical.* "One day, Jesus took James, John, and me aside and asked us to follow him. Since we had just sat down to rest, I admit we weren't too enthusiastic. The day was so hot, and here we were trudging up a dusty mountain path. As we climbed higher and higher, I felt like a furnace ready to explode. The sunlight bouncing off the rocks practically blinded me, and my mouth felt dry and gritty."
- *The emotional.* "Finally, we reached the top of the mountain. But Jesus didn't say anything—he just stood there. This whole thing was very puzzling! I was just about to ask Jesus what we were doing there when, suddenly, the mountaintop seemed to be on fire. Jesus' face became as dazzling as the sun, his clothes as radiant as light. And there, talking to him, were Moses and Elijah! Oh, my gosh, I was terrified. I fell to the ground. I didn't know what to do!"
- *The spiritual.* "The vision went as quickly as it had come. Later, as I thought about what happened, I knew I would never be the same again. Jesus was truly someone special, and he had chosen me to be a disciple. I knew then that no matter what, I would follow him—even if it meant my death."

After everyone has had a chance to present his or her story, encourage the group members to share how their own spiritual journeys have been like Peter's.

When the groups have finished, call them together and debrief the participants by discussing these questions:

- How do you see each episode to be a stage in Peter's spiritual growth?

- What have you learned about yourself from this activity?
- What does this activity suggest to you about the direction your life should take?

Variation

Summarizing the attitudes of Jesus and Peter. After each participant has role-played his or her selection about Peter, have each group print or write on a large sheet of newsprint a collage of words that express Jesus' attitude toward Peter and Peter's attitude toward Jesus. Then have the groups share and compare their collages. End the activity by using the last two debriefing questions listed above.

ACTIVITY 29
Role-Playing the Christmas Story

The people mentioned in the infancy narratives in the Gospels represent the different hopes and expectations of the people of Israel. This activity demonstrates how these narratives shed light on the mystery of Jesus and on the people's expectations of him.

Materials Needed

A Bible for each participant
Chalkboard or a display board
Variation 1: Costume materials, props, and Christmas music
Variation 2: Hand-puppet materials
Variation 3: Drawing paper and crayons for each participant

Procedure

Introduce the activity by saying, "In this activity, we are going to role-play the people mentioned in the infancy narratives. Each of you will be assigned a character or a group of characters and a Gospel passage. Read the passage and reflect on your character's hopes for the Messiah and his or her expectations of the kind of Messiah Jesus would be. Get in touch with the feelings your character must have had. When the reflection time is up, each of you, speaking in the first person, will tell the following: what role you had in the Christmas story, what you experienced, what the birth of Jesus meant to you, what you expected of him, and what effect the event had on your life."

To get the participants started, you may want to share the following example: "I am Simeon. I am old and tired. The Lord promised I would see the Messiah. I went every day to the temple to see him, but he never came. One day, this young couple came along. God spoke to me and told me that the child they carried was the Promised One. I was excited and praised God with all my heart. I knew that things would now be fine for Israel. I felt relieved and went home to die."

Check to make sure that everyone has a Bible, and then invite the participants to form groups of eight. While the participants are getting organized, write the following list on the chalkboard or a display board:

1. Angel Gabriel—Luke 1:26–28
2. Elizabeth—Luke 1:39–45
3. Joseph—Matthew 1:18–21, 2:19–23
4. The shepherds—Luke 2:8–18
5. The astrologers—Matthew 2:1–12
6. Simeon—Luke 2:22–35
7. Anna—Luke 2:36–38
8. Mary—Luke 1:38–55

As soon as everyone is settled, assign each group member a different character from the list. Allow at least ten minutes for the participants to get into their roles. Then have them take turns telling the other group members about their parts in the story and how they felt.

After they have finished, have the groups discuss the following questions:

- With which person or group in the Christmas story do you most closely identify? Why?
- How does your belief in the birth of Christ change the way you relate to others? Give two concrete examples.
- How did you feel while doing this activity? Did you get any new insights?

You may wish to end the activity by having the group sing one or two Christmas carols.

Variations

1. *Drama.* Ask one of the groups to act out the whole Christmas story. If you do this, provide appropriate costume materials, props, and music.
2. *Hand puppets.* Younger people might use hand puppets made from paper bags to tell the story of Jesus' birth. This method will reveal their real feelings and thoughts about the event.
3. *Gifts.* After reading the assigned Scripture passages, invite each participant to draw a picture of what his or her character would give as a gift to the Christ Child. The gift

should symbolize what the character expected Jesus to be and do. Afterward, each participant should explain his or her role in the story and present the gift to the Christ Child, explaining to the group what the gift symbolizes.

ACTIVITY 30
Interviewing Biblical Characters

It is not always easy to understand what Jesus was teaching in his parables. By using the simple, yet effective, interview technique, the participants go beyond the surface meaning of these powerful stories. In these interviews, the participants will really *feel* the message.

Materials Needed

A Bible for each participant
Chalkboard or a display board
A pencil and a sheet of writing paper for each group observer
A pencil and a copy of the interview and debriefing questions
    for each group reporter
Variation 3: A book on the lives of the saints, pencils, and
    writing paper

Procedure

Introduce the activity by saying, "The parables of Jesus are constantly challenging our lives. They are clues to what it means to be true followers of Jesus and children of God. But if we are to interpret the clues correctly we must read the stories with the eyes of faith and trust. In this activity, we will use the simple technique of interviewing to unravel the meaning of some of Jesus' stories. First, you will read one of the parables. Then, while some of you 'become' the characters in the story, others will play the role of a reporter. It is the reporter's job to find out not only what happened in the story but also what the characters' reactions and feelings were. Still others will play the role of a neutral outside observer who watches and reports on what occurs during the interviews. This process can help us have a better understanding of the message of Jesus and the kingdom of God."

Be sure that everyone has a Bible, and then invite the participants to form five groups. Check to see that each group has an equal number of participants. Ask for two volunteers from each group to play the roles of the reporter and the observer. If there is a certain amount of shyness among the participants, don't be afraid to appoint the "volunteers." Then assign one of the following Scripture passages to each group: Matthew 18:23–34 (the Merciless Official), Matthew 20:1–16 (the Laborers in the Vineyard), Luke 10:30–35 (the Good Samaritan), Luke 14:16–24 (the Great Feast), and Luke 15:11–32 (the Prodigal Son). The reporter in each group should then read aloud the passage to the group. After the reading, the reporter should assign a character from the story to each person in the group. Depending on the number of participants, it may be necessary for some group members to play more than one character. For example, the parable of the vineyard has a minimum of six characters: the owner of the vineyard, the worker hired at dawn, the worker hired at midmorning, the worker hired at noon, the worker hired at midafternoon, and the worker hired in late afternoon.

While the assignments are being made, write the following questions on the chalkboard or on a display board:

- What happened to your character?
- What did your character say or hear?
- How did your character feel about what happened?
- How did your character relate to the other people in the story?
- Did the story's events change your character? In what way?

As soon as everyone is ready, tell the participants to read their stories quietly and without discussion. They should use the questions on the board as a guide for their reflection. Tell the groups they have about ten minutes to complete this part of the activity.

During this reflection time, call the observers and the reporters aside, and outline their part in the activity. First, give the observers pencils and writing paper. Explain that during the interviews, they are to record their impressions of the characters and the main results of the questioning. At the end of the activity, they should be prepared to share their observations and insights.

Then, distribute pencils and copies of the interview sheet to the reporters. The interview sheet should contain two parts—the interview questions and the debriefing questions. Allow extra space between the interview questions in case the reporters want to jot down a few key words or to add questions of their own. The following is a list of possible interview questions:

- Will you tell us what you remember happening?
- Why did you respond the way you did?
- What was your attitude toward each of the other people?
- How did you feel about what happened?
- Have you had any reason to change your feelings or your attitudes?
- If you were given a chance to relive the situation, what would you do differently? Why?
- Do you feel you are better or worse for what happened? Why?
- Where do you go from here?

The second part of the interview sheet should list the following debriefing questions:

- What did you experience while playing this role?
- What did you gain from this activity?
- What message do you think Jesus is giving you through this story?

Explain to the reporters that it is their job to get the facts of the story and to shed a little light on each character's personality and viewpoint. While they should feel free to ask a character to clarify a response, they should not attempt to interpret or to inject their personal views.

When the reflection time is up, let the interviews begin. Remind the reporters to address each participant by his or her character name, and remind the participants to respond to all questions in the first person. As soon as the interviews are completed, the reporter should go right into the debriefing questions.

After the debriefing by the reporter, the observer should give his or her feedback, including any insights into the various characters and observations about the interviews.

Variations

1. *The life of Jesus.* Use the interview technique with the incidents in the life of Jesus rather than his parables. The following stories about Jesus lend themselves well to this

technique: the miracle of the loaves and fishes (John 6:1–15), the call of James and John (Mark 1:16–20), the call of Matthew (Matthew 9:9–13), the call of the rich young man (Matthew 19:16–22), the call of Saint Paul (Acts 9:1–9), the man possessed (Mark 5:1–20), and the blind Bartimaeus (Mark 10:46–52).

After the reporter asks various characters for the facts in the story—What happened? What kind of day was it? Where did the event take place? What were you doing at the time?—he or she should probe deeper and ask the main characters questions such as these:

- What had been going on in your life before your meeting with Jesus?
- How satisfied had you been with life up to this time?
- Where did you think your life was going before you met Jesus? after meeting him?
- How did this encounter change your life?

2. *The Apostles.* Another variation is to have the reporter interview the Apostles at various stages of their journey with Jesus. The same procedure as described above should be followed, but in this activity, the reporter should interview the same people at four different times in their lives. This variation lends itself to groups of six—the reporter, the observer, Peter, Andrew, James, and John. The following scenes should be considered: Galilee (Mark 1:16–22), Jerusalem after the death of Jesus (Mark 16:1–3), Jerusalem after the resurrection (Luke 24:13–21, John 20:19–25), and Pentecost (Acts 2:1–4).

When the group members have read and reflected on the Scripture passages, the reporter should ask each Apostle questions about how his life has been changed by the events and where he feels he is going. The observer should then give his or her feedback.

Finally, all the groups should come together and discuss the following debriefing questions:

- How did you feel during this activity?
- Did you experience the impact of Jesus on the life of the Apostle you were playing? How?
- Can you share a time in your own life when your hopes

or dreams were crushed and something good—even wonderful—came out of the experience?

- In what way do you feel that activities such as this are helpful in grasping the impact of Jesus on people and in understanding the Scriptures?

3. *The saints.* The interview technique can be used to learn more about the participants' favorite saints. Have each group read about an incident from the life of a saint, assign the roles, and allow the reporter to make up his or her own questions along the lines of those suggested in the activity and in Variations 1 and 2.

ACTIVITY 31
Dialoging with a Parable

The imagination is a wonderful faculty for unlocking a person's reactions and feelings. This kind of exercise turns the imagination loose on all the elements of a parable in order to elicit personal responses to the message of Jesus.

Materials Needed

A Bible
Writing paper and a pencil for each participant
Variation 2: Name tags

Procedure

Introduce the activity by saying, "A parable is a challenge to some aspect of our way of thinking or acting. Often that challenge is very obvious, but at other times, it takes a certain amount of reflection to see exactly how a particular parable is challenging us. In this activity, we will use our imaginations to have a dialog with the elements of the parable of the sower and the seed, and we'll see what surfaces."

Have the participants form groups of eight. To help the participants relax, ask them to take three or four deep breaths and slowly exhale after each one. Then have one of the participants read aloud Luke 8:5–8 to the whole group. After the reading, go around to each group and assign each group member a different element in the parable: the seed, the footpath, the birds, the rocky ground, the thorn bushes, the sun, the good soil, the farmer. Tell the participants that they will have ten minutes to have a silent dialog with their assigned elements and that they are not to talk with anyone in the group during this time. If they wish, they may write out their dialogs or make notes on them.

Before they begin, give the participants some general guidelines for the dialog:

1. Be sure the questions flow naturally.
2. Begin by asking the element about itself and what it does.
3. Describe how you are like the element.
4. Ask how you can relate to the other elements in the story.

To help the participants get started, you may wish to share the following sample questions:

- Tell me, Good Soil, what do you do?
- How did you become good soil?
- Who takes care of you, Good Soil, and how are you cared for?
- How do you help the farmer? the seeds? the birds?
- What can you do to become even better soil?

Then read aloud the parable once again, and have the participants begin their silent dialogs.

When ten minutes are up or when you see that everyone is finished, have the participants share their dialogs and then discuss what they see as the parable's major challenge. Encourage the participants to give examples of how they answer this challenge in their own lives. Afterward, call the groups together, and debrief the participants by discussing the following questions:

- What did you experience while doing this activity?
- What did you learn from this activity?

Close the session with a traditional prayer or a song from the Sunday liturgy.

Variations

1. *Other dialog parables.* The following stories also lend themselves well to the dialog technique: (a) the parable of the buried treasure (Matthew 13:44)—the elements would include the man, the treasure, the field, and all the other possessions; (b) the parable of the leaven (Matthew 13:13)—the elements would include the yeast, the flour, the dough, and the woman; (c) the parable of the mustard seed (Mark 4:30–32)—the elements would include the mustard seed, the soil, the shrub, the other plants, and the birds; (d) the parable of the good shepherd (Luke 15:4–6)—the elements would include the shepherd, the sheep, the wasteland, and the friends; and (e) the parable of the silver pieces (Luke 15:8–9)—the elements would include the woman, the silver pieces, the lamp, the broom, the house, and the friends.

2. *Playacting the dialogs.* Have each person wear a name tag telling which element in the story he or she is. Then have one "element"—for example, the farmer—carry on a dialog with another "element" in the story—for example, the birds. The farmer might ask the birds who they are, why they eat the seeds, what the seeds do for them, what they do for him, what they want, and how he and they might work together more closely. The birds can then ask similar questions of the farmer. Continue this procedure until all the elements have had a chance to dialog.

ACTIVITY 32
Eyewitness

Courtrooms and news reports are filled with the testimony of eyewitnesses. This kind of testimony relays more than facts. It also reveals the effect the event has on the eyewitness. In this activity, the participants get to act as eyewitnesses to the great act of redemption. They will reveal to the group the effect the suffering and death of Jesus had on them.

Materials Needed

A Bible, writing paper, and a pencil for each participant
A table and seven chairs for each group
Chalkboard or a display board
A candle and matches for each group
A small loaf of bread and a large cup of wine for each group
Background music

Procedure

Introduce the activity by saying, "In the years immediately following the death and resurrection of Jesus, the early Christians would gather together to hear about the way of Jesus and to celebrate the Lord's Supper. During these meals, the disciples—the eyewitnesses—would tell about the life of Jesus and his teachings. These stories gave shape and direction to the lives of the early Christians. These same stories can give shape and direction to our lives, too.

"In this activity, we are going to relive the passion and death of Jesus. But we are going to relive these events in a special way. We are going to pretend that we have experienced the events firsthand, that we are the eyewitnesses. And now, it is our job to share what we saw with others so that they too will believe in Jesus and know the peace of God's love."

Be sure that everyone has a Bible, and then ask the participants to form groups of seven. While the participants are gathering around the tables and getting settled, write the following list on the chalkboard or on a display board:

1. The agony in the garden—Matthew 26:36–46
2. Judas's betrayal—Matthew 26:20–25; 27:3–10

3. The arrest and trial of Jesus—Matthew 26:47–68
4. Peter's denial—Matthew 26:69–75
5. The trial before Pilate—Matthew 27:1–2, 11–26
6. The carrying of the cross and the crucifixion—Matthew 27:27–44
7. The death and burial of Jesus—Matthew 27:45–66

As soon as everyone is ready, pass out writing paper and a pencil to each group member, and assign him or her one of the stories listed on the board. Explain to the participants that they may use the paper to jot down key words or phrases to help them keep their stories on track. However, they should tell the stories in their own words, not read them. They should flesh out the stories with as many details as possible— the sounds, the colors, the feelings. Then tell the participants that they have about ten minutes to prepare their stories. Suggest that they work in silence.

As soon as the ten minutes are up, call time. Then, beginning with the first story listed on the board, have each group member tell his or her story. Remind the participants that they are eyewitnesses to the passion and death of Jesus and that they should tell their stories as dramatically as they can.

When all the stories have been told, go around to each group and place on the table a candle, matches, a cup of wine, and a loaf of bread. Ask someone in each group to light the candle, and then dim the room lights. Have the group members hold hands, and tell them to concentrate on the candle's flame as you read the following prayer: "Blessed are you, Lord, our God, for in the passion, death, and resurrection of Jesus, your Son, you have redeemed the world. May we, his followers, be more deeply united to him and to one another as we share these gifts of the earth."

Then have each group member break off a piece of bread and pass the loaf to the next person. As soon as everyone has a piece, the participants should eat the bread. The group members should then take turns drinking from the cup of wine. If possible, play appropriate background music during this time. After everyone has shared the bread and wine, turn up the lights and have the groups extinguish the candles.

Call all the groups together, and debrief the participants about the activity by discussing these questions:

- How did you feel while telling your story? while listening to the stories of others?
- What insights did you gain about the passion and death of Jesus?
- How were you affected by the experience?
- How are you feeling about the activity now?

ACTIVITY 33
Role-Playing the Past

The mature Christian realizes that life is too precious to waste. He or she does not spend time brooding about the past or refusing to set goals for the future. Instead, he or she lives fully in the present while maintaining a vision of both the past and the future. In this activity, the participants are given an opportunity to deal with past situations or problems so that they may live more fully in the present moment and move with greater freedom toward the future.

Materials Needed

Writing paper and a pencil for each participant

Procedure

Introduce the activity by saying, "We have heard over and over again that the past cannot be changed. In one sense, that is true; we cannot change the actual events that happened in the past. But in another sense, it is not true. We can change the *perception* of those events. If we can change the way we remember the past, we can gain new insights into the direction and meaning of our lives as well as a better understanding of our feelings and motives.

"One helpful way to look at the past in a new and more positive way is to role-play some important event from the past. The reenacted experience can be a good and pleasant one, or it can be a traumatic or even a distasteful one. By role-playing in a group, we can get to know and understand one another better because we will see, at least in this one instance, how we all think and react."

Distribute writing paper and pencils to the participants. Instruct everyone to think back over the past and to list three or four significant events in his or her life and the names of the people involved in those events. Then, when everyone has finished writing, ask for a volunteer who would be willing, with the help of the group, to role-play one of the events on his or her list. This event may be something as simple as beginning a new job or as traumatic as getting a divorce.

When someone has volunteered, ask how many players he or she will need for the role-play. For example, if the person wishes to role-play a divorce, he or she will probably need the former spouse, children, lawyers, in-laws, and so on.

After all the parts have been assigned, direct the participants to form a circle, with the role-players sitting in the center. Have the volunteer briefly describe the selected event and the roles of the other characters in the story. Then the volunteer should begin the role-play by telling what he or she said or did at the beginning of the experience. Those chosen to play roles should enter the conversation at the appropriate cues. Remind the players that this is more like improvisational theater than like reading a prepared script. The players may question, respond, argue, or agree, but they should always try to think and act like the people they are portraying.

When the skit is finished, ask for other volunteers, and repeat the process until everyone has had a chance to participate in a role-play. The option to pass should be available, however. Afterward, debrief the participants about the activity by discussing these questions:

- How did you feel while playing your part?
- What did you find the most difficult about the experience? the easiest?
- How did you feel about the other players and the roles they played?
- What are two things you learned about yourself from this experience?
- Did this experience help change your feelings or understanding of a past incident in any way? If so, how?

6
Praying

Each person is unique and has a special relationship with God, with others, and with self. Prayer is a very important way of getting in touch with these relationships. One Church Father has said that people cannot pray for long without confronting themselves, and that prayer will lead people to the heart of God, who will fill them with love and compassion for their neighbor.

Prayer has been described in many ways. It is lifting one's mind and heart to God, listening to God, talking to God, putting oneself in the presence of God. In the Christian tradition, there are many methods of prayer, and most of them are still valid. No one method is the best for all people. Many find, for example, that the step-by-step Ignatian method of meditation on a Scripture reading is helpful, while others prefer a less discursive method of prayer based on Scripture readings. The following activities offer a variety of methods for using Scripture as a basis for prayer.

WHAT TO EXPECT

By using the activities in this chapter, the participants will see that there is more than one way to use the Bible in prayer. When they share their unique prayer experiences with one another, they gain an understanding of the different ways that God is active in the world, and they are better able to grasp the meaning of God's Word for themselves. Through this sharing, they are better able to see God's vision for their lives and God's plan for the group.

Praying together is an excellent way to build Christian community. It allows the group to discern God's presence among them and God's plan for them as a group. Communal prayer often enriches personal prayer but requires practice for many people. Both communal and personal prayer challenge people to grow.

- Activity 34, "Shared Bible Prayer," helps the participants share their thoughts and feelings about a particular biblical passage and leads them into common prayer.
- Activity 35, "The Lord's Prayer," helps the group discover the personal meaning of the petitions of the Lord's Prayer and use these as a basis for prayer.
- Activity 36, "Reflecting in a Group," challenges the participants to reflect on their recent experiences of Christ and to pray together about these experiences.
- Activity 37, "Guided Meditation," leads the participants through a meditation in which they use imagination rather than reasoning.
- Activity 38, "Praying with New Vision," helps the participants see their life situations more clearly.
- Activity 39, "Using Music to Pray," uses popular records or tapes as an occasion of prayer.
- Activity 40, "Linking Up," stresses the power of group prayer.

INTENDED AUDIENCE

These activities can be used in any number of situations with practically any group. They fit in especially well with a day of recollection or a retreat, and they can easily be used in conjunction with other activities in the book.

ACTIVITY 34
Shared Bible Prayer

There are many occasions when groups may wish to pray together using the Bible. A variety of methods for doing this
will keep the group from getting into a rut and feeling that
there is only one way to use the Bible in prayer. This activity
suggests four ways in which a biblical passage can be read,
reflected upon, shared, and prayed over.

Materials Needed

A Bible for each participant

Procedure

Because this activity will probably be used as part of a day of
recollection or in conjunction with a special meeting, you
will have to tailor the introduction to the situation. In all
cases, the procedure is very similar. Have the participants sit
in a circle and take a few moments to quiet down and become
recollected. Then follow one of the following methods.

Method 1. Ask a volunteer to read the Gospel selection for
the coming Sunday or another appropriate Scripture passage.
Then invite each participant to share with the group what the
passage means to him or her. After the sharing, ask another
volunteer to read the passage aloud a second time, and ask
each person to share what new insights he or she received
from the second reading. Finally, have the passage read aloud
a third time. Invite the participants to express their thoughts
and feelings in spontaneous, vocal prayer.

Method 2. Have the participants read an assigned Scripture
passage to themselves and underline the words that strike
them. After the reading, invite the participants to share the
words they underlined and to tell the thoughts, feelings, and
experiences these words brought to mind. Then have one of
the participants read the passage slowly and prayerfully to the
group. Ask the participants to express in prayer, either aloud
or silently, the thoughts and feelings that surfaced during the
final reading.

Method 3. Sometime before the session begins, select one
of your favorite Scripture passages to share with the group.

When the participants are ready, tell them to listen carefully as you read the passage aloud. They are to select one or two phrases that are particularly meaningful to them. When you have finished reading the passage, have the participants take turns sharing the phrases that struck them. There should be no discussion of the participants' choices, but be sure to allow a slight pause between speakers. As soon as everyone has had a chance to share, read the Scripture selection a second time. Invite the participants to express in vocal prayer what is running through their minds.

Method 4. Have the participants gather in a circle with their Bibles, and ask them to choose one or two favorite verses. If you wish, limit the selections to one particular book in the Bible. Be available to help those who have difficulty making a choice.

After each person reads his or her verse, allow a fifteen- to thirty-second pause so that the group can reflect on God's message. Then ask the participants to share their thoughts and feelings about the reading. Conclude the activity by inviting spontaneous prayers.

ACTIVITY 35
The Lord's Prayer

The Lord's Prayer is a direct and personal lesson in how to pray. This exercise helps the participants break open the prayer and take the lesson to heart. This technique helps make one of the most familiar prayers in the world fresh and new.

Materials Needed

Chalkboard or a display board
A copy of the Activity Worksheet for each participant
Writing paper, two index cards, and a felt-tipped marker for
   each group

Procedure

Invite the participants to say the Lord's Prayer slowly and thoughtfully. As the group recites the prayer, write the following phrases on the chalkboard or on a display board: *thy kingdom come, give us this day our daily bread, lead us not into temptation,* and *deliver us from evil.* Explain to the participants that in this activity, they are going to concentrate on these four phrases so that they can learn to say the Lord's Prayer in a fresh and new way.

Then ask the participants to form groups of four, and give each group member a copy of the Activity Worksheet. Review the Worksheet directions and tell the participants they have about ten minutes to complete their work.

When everyone has finished writing, have each group pick a recorder, and give the recorder writing paper, two index cards, and a marker. As the participants share their Worksheet answers, the recorder should keep track of the responses. After everyone has had a chance to share, the participants can use the list of responses to compose two prayers of the faithful. The recorder should write the prayers on the index cards.

Then ask the groups to gather together and to form a circle. Have the recorders take turns reading aloud the prayers. After each prayer, the group should say "Lord, hear our prayer." Conclude the activity by saying or singing the Lord's Prayer together.

Variations

1. *Reflecting on the life of the group.* Instead of having the participants reflect on their individual lives, have them reflect on the four phrases from the Lord's Prayer in relation to the life of the group. Have them consider, for example, what the dangers to the group are and what things have made them realize that God's kingdom has come into the life of the group.

2. *Reflecting on the life of the family.* This activity can be used effectively with individual families or with groups of families. Give a copy of the Worksheet to one of the adults in the family, and have him or her read the questions aloud. Tell the adult leader to rephrase the questions in terms of the family instead of individuals. The leader should also appoint someone in the group to record the responses on the Worksheet. After everyone has had a chance to share, the family should then write a prayer of the faithful. This prayer can be used at mealtime or as a family night prayer. The leader should conclude the activity by asking the family members to hold hands and to say or sing the Lord's Prayer.

WORKSHEET
The Lord's Prayer

Often people recite the Lord's Prayer without reflecting on its meaning. Below are a series of questions to help you personalize this prayer. Write the responses to these questions in the space provided.

1. What two recent events have helped you realize that God's kingdom has come into your life?

2. What are two or three things you need as daily bread?

3. What are one or two temptations you face?

4. What evils do you want to be delivered from?

ACTIVITY 36
Reflecting in a Group

Sometimes, parish groups become so task-oriented that the members forget to take the time to reflect on God's presence in their own lives. This activity can help these groups step back, observe their spiritual growth, and pray together.

Procedure

When the time has come for the group to pray, suggest that the participants spend a little quiet time reflecting on a moment during the meeting or since the last meeting when they experienced Christ's presence.

After a period of reflection, invite each person to share his or her moment with the group. When each person has finished sharing, ask the others if they have any feedback or insights for the person. For example, they might share how this person's experience has affected them or they might reflect on how they see the person growing.

After this sharing, ask the participants to pray aloud spontaneously, praising and thanking God.

ACTIVITY 37
Guided Meditation

This activity presents a model for you to use in creating guided meditations. This type of meditation helps participants use their imagination to get in touch with Christ and to look at their own lives. Almost any Scripture story may be used in this manner. John 1:35–39, Mark 1:40–42, and Mark 10:46–52 are especially good choices.

Materials Needed

A Bible
Writing paper and a pencil for each participant
Tape recorder and blank tape (optional)

Procedure

Note to the facilitator: It is important that you read the meditation slowly, pausing briefly after each new direction to allow the participants time to form an image in their minds or to follow the directions. Prior to using the meditation with the group, you may want to practice reading it aloud to another person. He or she can critique your delivery and help you determine whether or not you are reading the meditation too quickly. Mark the words where you want to pause. Places requiring a longer than usual break are noted in the text. You may also choose to tape-record the meditation and critique yourself. If you use this method, feel free to play the taped version for your group and to join in the meditation.

Introduce the activity by asking the participants to seat themselves at a reasonable distance from one another and to get comfortable. Tell them that this form of prayer requires them to be quiet and relaxed so that their imaginations can work freely. Begin by reading aloud John 21:1–17. Pause a few moments after the reading. Then read the following meditation.

"Now that you are all comfortable, I want you to close your eyes. Keep them closed until I ask you to open them. Take a deep breath, filling your lungs. Let it out slowly, and begin to feel yourself relax. Once more fill your lungs with a deep breath. Hold it. Now let it out slowly. Feel your body relaxing more and more.

"Let this wonderful feeling of relaxation flow all the way down to your feet. Allow it to flow up to your ankles. Feel it going up through the large and small muscles of your legs to your knees. With every breath you exhale, you feel more relaxed and comfortable.

"Now let this feeling of relaxation flow from your knees into your thighs, from your thighs into your hips, from your hips into your abdomen. With every breath you exhale, your body just keeps on relaxing more and more.

"Let this wonderful feeling of relaxation flow up into the large and small muscles of your back. Go limp as a rag doll. Let the feeling of relaxation flow up into your shoulders and down into your chest, such a wonderful, comfortable feeling. And with every breath you exhale, your body is relaxing more and more.

"Now let the feeling of relaxation flow down the muscles of your arms to your elbows, to your wrists, from your wrists into your hands, right on to the ends of your fingers. With each breath you exhale, you feel more relaxed.

"Let the feeling of relaxation flow up all the large muscles of your neck. Let it come to your head. Let it flow down into your brow. The muscles of your eyes are relaxing. The muscles of your chin are relaxing. All the tension is leaving your face. You are completely relaxed.

"Now picture an elevator in front of you. The door opens. You step in. The door closes. You begin to descend. Ten, nine, eight. You are going deeper. Seven, six, five. Deeper. Four, three, two. Let yourself go. Relax. One, zero. The door opens and you step out.

"You are on the shore of a lake. It is early morning and the sun is up. The air is warm with sweet fragrances all around you. Birds are singing. Water is lapping at the shore.

"You have finished eating. You are relaxed and comfortable. Other people are near you. Jesus is here. You look intently at him as he walks up to you. He is standing in front of you. You look at him. He looks at you.

"He calls you by name and says, 'Do you love me?' (*Pause for about 20 seconds.*)

"You respond. (*Pause about 15 seconds.*)

"A second time he calls you by name and asks, 'Do you love me?' (*Pause about 10 seconds.*)

"A second time you respond.

"A third time he calls you by name and asks, 'Do you love me?' (*Pause 10 or 15 seconds.*)

"You respond.

"Jesus then says, 'Feed my sheep.' You listen to his voice. (*Pause about 30 seconds.*)

"Slowly Jesus turns and walks away from you. You turn and enter the door of the elevator. The elevator begins to ascend. One, two, three, four. You are feeling loved. Five, six. You feel peaceful and refreshed. Seven. This is going to be a wonderful day. Eight. You are beginning to wake now. Nine, ten. Open your eyes. You are fully awake and back in the room."

Give the participants a few moments to get reacclimated to their surroundings. Then give them writing paper and pencils, and have them write down their immediate reactions to the meditation. When everyone has finished writing, ask the participants to form small groups and to share their reactions.

Debrief the participants about the experience by asking questions such as these:

- How did you enjoy the meditation?
- What struck you during the meditation?
- What was the best part of the meditation for you?
- Did you receive any insights or inspirations during the meditation?
- Do you think you can use this type of relaxing meditation by yourself? If so, when?

ACTIVITY 38
Praying with New Vision

The following prayer activity is based on everyone's need to look at life from a different perspective. The participants are invited to soar over their everyday circumstances to see how they can grow and change.

Materials Needed

A large sheet of newsprint and a colored marker for each participant

Procedure

Introduce the activity by saying, "Listen carefully to this passage from the Book of Isaiah: 'They who hope in the Lord will renew their strength, and they will soar as with eagles' wings' (40:31). When we pray and reflect in God's presence, we can get a different view of the way things are. The Scripture passage speaks of soaring above our everyday circumstances and getting a new view of our lives—a bird's-eye view."

Invite the participants to get comfortable and then continue with the following meditation: "What you are about to experience is a prayer—a special meditation. Close your eyes for a moment and listen to my voice. Relax your body. Imagine yourself rising above your home, the neighborhood, the city. See how it is laid out. See the people moving around, your family and friends. See the good that is there—the love of the people. See the problems that exist—the pain, the need for forgiveness and healing. Let your mind drift over the situation, rising higher and higher for a better view."

After an appropriate amount of time, tell the participants to open their eyes. Then pass out sheets of newsprint and colored markers to the group. Have each participant draw one thing he or she saw that needs to be changed. Below the drawing, the participant should write a short prayer asking for God's healing love.

As soon as everyone has finished writing, have the participants form small groups and share their work. Conclude the activity by asking the participants to join hands and to say the Lord's Prayer.

ACTIVITY 39
Using Music to Pray

Popular music is often filled with the joys and sorrows of human life. This activity helps the participants find a source of real prayer in music.

Materials Needed

A phonograph or tape player
A record or tape of popular songs
A Bible for each participant

Procedure

Have the participants get comfortable, and ask them to close their eyes. Play a popular song for the group. If the participants are young, choose one of the Top 40 songs. If it is an adult group, you might want to use one of the standards. A country and western song would probably work well with any age group. Whichever song you select, be sure it deals with some aspect of relationships.

After playing the song, ask the group to discuss the following questions:

- What is the person who is singing the song feeling?
- What is the relationship that the person is struggling with?
- What qualities of prayer do you find in this song?
- How can this song lead one to pray?

Then ask each participant to find a story in the Scriptures that reflects the same feelings heard in the song. Be available to help those who have difficulty selecting an appropriate story.

Have the participants take turns sharing their stories. Then play the song again, and allow some time for silent meditation. Afterward, invite the participants to pray about their experiences of the song and the Scripture sharing.

ACTIVITY 40
Linking Up

Prayer can also be found in tactile, physical expression. In this activity, the participants use modeling clay to create a common prayer of petition.

Materials Needed

Modeling clay for each participant
A table
Variation: Strips of paper and glue

Procedure

Introduce the activity by saying, "There is great power when we come together to pray. Jesus said that where two or three are gathered in his name, he is present. We all pray for things that we want or need. We are now going to do this as a group."

Distribute modeling clay to each participant. Explain to the group that each participant should select one thing he or she has recently prayed for and "mold" the petition in clay. Remind the group that this is not an art class—any and all attempts are acceptable.

When everyone has finished his or her model, ask the participants to share their creations with the group. After the first presentation, the participant should put his or her clay creation on the table in the center of the group. The next person who shares should attach his or her model to the first one, and so on. When all the participants have shared and joined their pieces of clay, allow time for spontaneous prayer.

Variation

Paper links. Instead of clay, use one-by-ten-inch strips of paper. Have each participant write a specific need or problem on a strip of paper. After the first person shares, he or she should join the ends of the strip of paper with some quick-drying glue to form a loop. The next person who shares should then put his or her paper through the first loop and glue the ends to start a chain. Continue this procedure until everyone has had a chance to share. Allow time for spontaneous prayer.

7

Celebrating

A celebration is an event that involves more than a discussion or a talk. It is a way of getting in touch with oneself by bringing together different aspects of one's life and seeing them in a broader context. It involves the total person—the five senses as well as the artistic, the imaginative, the kinesthetic, and the spiritual senses.

The activities in this chapter focus on concrete objects suggested by the Scriptures. They allow the objects, in personified form, to speak to the participants about their lives, their journeys, and their relationships to God and to others. The participants use all of their senses to encounter these objects which then serve as catalysts for reflection and a sharing of faith.

WHAT TO EXPECT

The activities open new doors of self-understanding for the participants, and combine prayer and healing with this new image of self. This combination can lead to personal change, to the growth of self-esteem, and to a renewed commitment to God and others.

Through these activities, the participants will explore some of the brokenness in their lives and have an opportunity to heal some of their wounds. Some participants may experience deep emotions and find it easy to express them. Others may become conscious of feelings they have repressed for years and are reluctant to share them. Whatever the participants' initial reactions are, the activities can help the group experience a sense of community and God's healing love.

- Activity 41, "Healing Your Hurts," uses small rocks to help the participants become aware of life's hurts and heal them.
- Activity 42, "Following the Light," uses light as a symbol of reconciliation to God and to others.
- Activity 43, "Planting a Seed," uses a seed to help participants discover and activate the dormant parts of their lives.
- Activity 44, "Molding Your Life in Clay," uses clay as a means of removing the impurities in the participants' lives—impurities that prevent God from being their potter.
- Activity 45, "Exchanging Coins for Life," uses coins to help participants see that clinging to things keeps them from following Christ.

INTENDED AUDIENCE

In general, these activities work best with people who have already developed a sense of trust and openness. They can also be effectively used to help people get in touch with their feelings or express them to others. People who are dealing with divorce, death in the family, strained relationships, or some unresolved problem will also profit from the activities. If you wish, use one or more of the activities as a preparation for the sacrament of Penance.

ACTIVITY 41
Healing Your Hurts

This activity helps the participants see how the hurts in their lives prevent them from connecting to their inner selves, to other people, and to God. By symbolically transferring these hurts from their hearts to external objects, the participants can gain a sense of new life and freedom.

Materials Needed

A small table
A candle and matches
A large metal trash can
A bowl of water, a towel, and a container of oil
A tape player or phonograph
Recorded music used for communal penance
Two fist-sized rocks for each participant
A Bible

Procedure

Just before the participants arrive, arrange their chairs in a circle. Include a chair for yourself. Put a small table in front of your chair and center a candle on the table. Place a large trash can at your left, situating it between you and the nearest participant. Nearby, put a bowl of water, a towel, and a container of oil. A tape player or a phonograph should be in a convenient spot. Preset the volume on low. Place two rocks for each participant on a pile in the middle of the circle.

When the group is assembled, introduce the activity by saying, "This activity will open new doors of understanding. It will help us experience some of the brokenness in our lives and give us an opportunity to heal some of those wounds. Now, each of you pick up two rocks from the pile and return to your seat."

When everyone is seated, light the candle and dim the room lights. Tell the participants to hold one rock in each hand. Then say, "Take a few moments to get to know your rocks. Feel their hardness, their coldness, their weight. Turn them over, and feel all aspects of them. Reflect on how these rocks are like you. There are parts of you that are rough, parts that are hard, parts that are worn down."

After a brief pause, play a song that speaks of God's intimate knowledge of our lives. Then say, "Hold the rocks in your lap. These rocks are the burdens of your life. They are the wounds you carry. Some are of your own making. Others have been laid on you by life. Let yourself feel the weight of these burdens. Locate the part of your body that carries these burdens, the part of your body that hurts. Get in touch with the hurt inside. These unhealed hurts are blocks to living in the present."

Give some examples of the types of hurts that people experience. These examples should be directed to the particular needs of the group. The following will help you:

1. You were lost in a large family.
2. You were bullied and developed a fear of others.
3. At school, you couldn't live up to the expectations of others and began to feel stupid.
4. Your parents were always fighting, or perhaps they were alcoholics. You felt helpless and alone.
5. Maybe you have been hurt by your own sins, times when you have used or abused someone you love.

During this part of the activity, be sure the participants feel free to vent their feelings. Do not allow the group to rescue those who are in pain. If someone wants to interrupt with a helpful suggestion, gently remind the person that this is a time to listen, not to play Ann Landers.

After an appropriate time for quiet reflection, say, "Now that you are in touch with your hurt, slowly allow the burden to move through your body and flow into the rocks. Feel it begin to move. Allow it to flow down your head and down your arms. Now feel it flowing through your hands into the rocks. Become conscious of how the rocks feel. Slowly let the burden of your life, the pain, enter into the rocks."

Then ask the participants to stand and to hold out their rocks in front of them. Say, "Brothers and sisters, in coming together, we have brought with us the cares and burdens of our lives. Some of these were laid upon us by life. Others are of our own making. Some we call misfortunes. Others we call sins. Let us reflect for a moment not only on those troubles that tire and discourage us but also on those faults and weaknesses that weigh us down."

Pause for about thirty seconds, and then ask the participants to choose a partner. Tell the partners to hold their rocks so that they touch. Then say slowly, "Our burdens make us weary. We want to reach out, to touch and nourish others, but our burdens and cares get in the way. We reach out, but we never really touch each other. Our weakness and our faults keep us from really feeling the warmth and love of others. Often there is so much that comes between us."

After a few moments of meditation, ask the participants to sit and to hold their rocks against their hearts. Then slowly say, "Our burdens and our cares keep us from really being in touch with ourselves, with our own feelings. Sometimes we are troubled, lonely, and uncertain. We live with unspoken secrets, with hearts burdened with mistrust. Our hearts are not free to speak of the love they contain for ourselves and for others." Then read Ezekiel 36:24–30 to the group.

After the reading, tell the participants, "Extend your arms, and rest your hands on your knees, still holding your rocks." While the participants are in this position, read Matthew 11:28–30 to the group.

Afterward, say the following litany, "Lord, we want to do your work, but you know how easily we grow weary. We want to reach you, but our faults and weaknesses keep us from touching you. Our hope and trust are in your mercy that touches us and says to us, 'Yes, you are forgiven. Yes, keep trying.' Lord, have mercy.

"Lord Jesus, you taught us to forgive as we want to be forgiven and to love as you have loved us. So many troubles, so many selfish ways, so many fears come between us. It is hard to trust and touch each other. Help us keep trying. Help us forgive and love each other. Christ have mercy.

"Lord, you know how difficult it is to really be in touch with ourselves. We are troubled, lonely, and uncertain. Sometimes it is so hard to live with unspoken secrets and fears, to forgive our hidden faults. Help us love ourselves as you love us. Free our hearts to move with the Spirit and find our peace in saying, 'Yes, I'll keep trying. Yes, I am loved.' Lord have mercy."

When the prayer is finished, tell the person on your left to drop his or her rocks into the trash can. Then have the participants pass their rocks to the right, and the person on your left should keep dropping the rocks into the trash can until all the rocks have been thrown away. (The rocks should be dropped so that there is a loud noise.)

Then take the towel and the bowl of water, and give each person a chance to wash and dry his or her hands. While this is being done, play some appropriate background music.

After the hands of all participants have been washed, silently anoint with oil the palms of the person on your left. (The music may continue.) That person should then anoint the hands of the person on his or her left, and so on. Then say, "Our hands and hearts are now free to touch and build, to help and to love God, our neighbors, and ourselves. Let us take this moment to offer one another a sign of peace."

Have the participants exchange the sign of peace, and then let them talk about the experience. If necessary, use these questions:

- What did you experience as you put your burden into the rocks?
- How did you feel when you held out your rocks in front of you?
- What did you feel when you held your rocks against those of another person? against your heart?
- What did you experience as you passed your rocks?
- What did you experience when you washed your hands?
- Did you experience any significant change or reaction as a result of this activity?

ACTIVITY 42
Following the Light

The symbol of light is an ancient and powerful part of believing. Jesus called his followers to be "lights of the world." This activity can help the participants pass from darkness to light.

Materials Needed

A small table, matches, and a candle inscribed with a symbol
    of Christ
One candle for each participant
Parish hymnals
A Bible
Background music

Procedure

Just before the participants arrive, arrange the chairs in a circle. Light a candle and put it on a table in the middle of the circle. When everyone has assembled, introduce the activity by saying, "This celebration is going to help us get in touch with ourselves through the imagery and symbolism of light. We all have experienced what it means to say 'I see!' when we finally understand how to solve a problem. On the other hand, when we are puzzled or lost, we may say, 'I'm in the dark!' This celebration is like the candle on this table. It can shed light on ourselves and our relationships with which we are not totally at peace. It will help us recognize where we need to be reconciled so that we can be a light for others."

Give each person a lighted candle, and dim the room lights. Ask the participants to focus their attention on the candle flame. Say quietly and slowly, "Light gives us the ability to see. It is warm. It provides security. It is life-giving. It is one of the ways Saint John described Jesus and those who follow him."

Then distribute copies of the parish hymnal, and have the participants sing a song about Christ being the light of the world. Then say, "O God, you are a God of light. At the beginning of creation, you made the sun to light the day and the moon to brighten the night. You made your people to walk in light. In the fullness of time, you sent your Son, Jesus, to be the light of the world. He came to brighten the hearts of all who believe in you so that they would no longer live in darkness and fear but in the joy of new life. We who follow Jesus often find ourselves struggling with the darkness. We do not always see clearly the path we are to follow. Help us with your light so that we may again see clearly and reflect the light of your love to others."

After a short pause, invite the participants to turn to one or two others and share their answers to the following questions:

- How is the candle you hold like a person?
- How is this candle like you?

When the discussions begin to wind down, call the group back together and ask for some brief feedback. Then read Matthew 5:14–16 to the group. Ask the participants to reflect silently on the following two questions:

- What are some of the bushel baskets in your life?
- What keeps your light hidden and prevents you from giving praise to your heavenly Father?

After a few moments, tell the participants that you are going to name some people who play an important part in their lives. If there is darkness in a relationship you mention, they are to blow out their candles. Then begin to name some common relationships—for example, father, mother, husband, wife, children, brothers, sisters, boss, best friend. Pause for a few moments after each suggestion. At the end of the list, all the candles will have been blown out, and only the "Christ" candle on the table will still be lit.

Ask the participants to focus on the candle's light, and say, "We all have dark spots in our lives. Our light is not always shining. We need the light of Christ, for his light never fades. He is the light of the world. Only Christ can restore our light and help us be his light to others. Let us take a few minutes and ask him to forgive us and to give us his light again."

After a few moments, say the following prayer: "Lord Jesus, you came so that we could walk in the light and reflect your light to others. Sometimes we fail to be the light and encouragement a loved one needs. We ask for your forgiveness. Help us love others from our hearts and not resent or mistrust them. We ask this in your name. Amen." Encourage the participants to add their own petitions for light.

If there are to be confessions, invite the participants to receive the sacrament of Penance. If not, ask them to reflect on ways they might heal a troubled relationship. After receiving the sacrament or making a quiet meditation, each participant should relight his or her candle from the Christ candle. If you wish, play some quiet background music during this time.

Afterward, read Ephesians 5:8–21 to the group, and say the following prayer: "Lord, we thank you for restoring light to our lives. Help us follow Jesus, the light of the world. Let his light shine in our lives to heal a broken world. Amen."

Conclude the activity by having the participants sing an appropriate song from their hymnals and then share the sign of peace.

ACTIVITY 43
Planting a Seed

In rural communities, planting time is really a great statement of hope. Farmers abandon their seed to the ground in the expectation of a great harvest. In this activity, the participants use real seed as a symbol of their own potential for growth and change.

Materials Needed

A table, potting soil, and a small plastic cup for each
 participant
A seed for each participant
A copy of the Activity Worksheet and a pencil for each
 participant
Parish hymnals
A Bible

Procedure

Before the participants arrive, arrange their chairs in a circle. In the center of the circle, place a table and on the table, potting soil and a small plastic cup for each participant. When the group is assembled, give each participant a seed. Then tell the following story: "When King Tut's tomb was discovered in 1922, it had been sealed for over five thousand years. Among the contents of the tomb were several containers of wheat—food for the king in his afterlife. Someone had the idea of planting some of this wheat to see if it would still germinate. With a little water and sun, the seeds quickly sprouted and came to life. These grains of wheat contained the power of life. At the right time and under the right circumstances, they came to life. The power was in them all the time but was dormant.

"Human beings are very much like seed. God has placed a dream and a longing for a fuller life within each person. Parts of that dream lie dormant for many years—sometimes remaining buried and forgotten. At the same time, each person experiences a longing for a more abundant life. One of the requirements for the fulfillment of the dream is the right environment for that dream to come to life and grow.

183

"The right environment includes a recognition that people can grow, the ability to express this longing, support from others, and a personal willingness to take the risk of planting, dying, and coming to a new life."

Have the participants examine their seed and reflect for a few moments on how they are like a seed. Then pass out copies of the Activity Worksheet, and ask the participants to fill it out. When everyone has finished writing, have the participants form small groups and share their answers. After about twenty minutes, distribute copies of the parish hymnal, and have the participants sing a song which reflects the theme of this activity. (Most hymnals have songs about spiritual growth.)

Then read Matthew 13:31–32 to the group, and ask the participants to look at their seed. Say, "Great things have small beginnings. The same power that was in the mustard seed is in the small seed that you hold. Part of you is like the seed. It is dormant, but there is a spark of greatness there. Reflect on the part of you that you would like to see come to life and grow." Pause for a few moments of reflection.

Then invite each person to go to the table and to plant his or her seed in one of the cups. Encourage the participants to share their dreams. After each person plants his or her seed, the group can respond, "Lord, help (the participant's name) to grow." Conclude the activity by having the group sing an appropriate song from the hymnal.

Variations

1. *Using another parable.* Instead of the parable of the mustard seed, use the parable of the sower (Matthew 13:4–9). Have the participants form small groups and share their responses to the questions on the Activity Worksheet. Then ask the groups to discuss these additional questions:

   - What are the obstacles in your life that make you like the footpath? the rocky ground? the thorn bushes?
   - What qualities do you have that make you like the good soil?

2. *Analyzing the work of a group.* A parish group or organization can use this activity to examine its reason for exist-

ence. Instead of using the Activity Worksheet, have the group discuss the following questions:

- What lies dormant in our group that needs to take root and come to new life?
- What are some of the steps we need to take in order to create the right environment for growth in these areas?
- What are some of the obstacles we need to overcome in order for this growth to occur?
- What did you learn from this experience?

WORKSHEET
Planting a Seed

Write a brief response to each question below. Do not spend a lot of time thinking about the questions. You will be closer to the truth if you jot down the first things that come to mind.

1. What hopes and dreams lie dormant in you?

2. What can you do to make these hopes and dreams come to life?

3. What risks do you need to take?

4. What can the group do to help you grow?

ACTIVITY 44
Molding Your Life in Clay

It isn't easy to let God take charge over one's life. Often, even the most ardent Christian acts like a bad lump of clay— fighting the potter's hands. In this activity, the participants themselves work with clay in order to recognize more easily God's action in their lives.

Materials Needed

A two-ounce ball of clay, a pebble, and a plastic bag for each
   participant
A table, a small tray, a candle, and matches
A Bible
Parish hymnals
A pan of water and towels

Procedure

Before the session begins, prepare a small ball of clay for each participant. Stick a pebble into the clay, and put the clay in a plastic bag so it doesn't dry out. Arrange the participants' chairs in a circle, and place a table in the center of the circle. On the table, place a candle, a tray, and the balls of clay. When everyone has arrived, give each participant a ball of clay, light the candle, and dim the room lights.

Introduce the activity by saying, "The Scriptures often speak of God as a potter and humankind as the potter's clay. We will use our clay to help us realize more clearly that God continues to mold and shape our lives through the Scriptures and the events of our lives. Sometimes, we may resist this process. We want to be the potter. We want to shape our own lives. But it is only by surrendering our lives to God that we can become all God created us to be.

"Before we begin, we need to understand the way in which potters prepare and mold clay. They begin by kneading. They move the clay between their hands and fingers, they get to know the characteristics of the clay—how soft or firm, how rough or smooth, how pliable or rigid. Each piece of clay is unique. Each has its own potential and stress points.

"As potters apply pressure to the clay, they feel out and eliminate any pockets of trapped air. In the heat of the kiln, air pockets would expand and shatter a piece of pottery. Potters also continually feel for small stones or bits of gravel. These must be removed before the clay can be properly formed.

"When the clay is ready, potters place it on a wheel to be shaped. They lubricate the clay with oil so that it will slide in their hands without friction. The clay must be perfectly centered on the wheel. If it is off center, it will resist and not be easy to shape. Once the clay is centered, spinning true and properly lubricated, potters simply find the vertical axis of the clay, press their thumbs down on the clay, and begin to shape the vessel.

"When potters are finished, they set the vessel aside to dry and then coat it with a glaze to give it color. The vessel is now ready to be fired. When the vessel has been heated to the proper temperature and fired, it is completed. Then it is removed from the kiln and cooled. The vessel is now ready to be used."

Read Jeremiah 18:1–6 to the group. If you wish, follow this reading with a familiar song from the parish hymnal.

Then have the participants take their clay out of the bags. Say the following instructions slowly: "Get to know your clay. Feel its texture, its temperature, its smoothness. Begin to shape it. Let your imagination flow with the clay. God is the potter. You are the clay. How are you like this lump of clay? How have the events and pressures of life shaped you? How have you tried to mold your own life? How centered in God are you?

"Now remove the pebble from your clay. The pebble is an impurity, a flaw that prevents the clay from being molded. What in your life is like this pebble? What keeps you from being molded by God? How do you resist allowing God to shape your life?"

If this activity is part of the sacrament of Penance, invite the participants to take their pebbles to the confessor and to share with him what the pebbles represent in their lives. When he gives them absolution, they should give him their pebbles.

If the activity is not part of the sacrament, have the participants put their pebbles on the tray as it is passed around.

Each person should tell, in some vague or general way, what the pebble represents. Then place the tray of pebbles on the table, and say this prayer: "Lord, you are the potter, and we are the clay, the work of your hands. There are many things in our lives that resist being molded by you and your love. There are many pebbles in our lives. We want to remove these pebbles so that we may truly be your people. Forgive us for having kept these obstacles alive in our lives. We give up these pebbles now as a sign that we want to allow you to shape our lives. Give us the new life of your Son, Jesus. Amen."

Then ask the participants to mold their clay into symbols of what they hope to have grow in their lives. As the group is working, remove the tray of pebbles from the table. When everyone has finished, invite the participants to put their symbols on the table next to the candle. As each person places his or her symbol, the group should say, "Let God mold you!"

Conclude the activity by having the group sing a familiar song from the parish hymnal. After the song, say, "Go now, and let God's Word form you and mold your lives." (If possible, provide water and towels so that the participants can wash their hands.)

ACTIVITY 45
Exchanging Coins for Life

The miser's tight fist is a symbol of a person who lacks the generosity and openness it takes to grow. In this activity, the participants use coins and the clenched fist as part of a celebration of their need to let go!

Materials Needed

A small table, a can, matches, and a candle inscribed with a
   symbol of Christ
A large metal pan
Two coins for each participant
A Bible
A sheet of writing paper and a pencil for each participant
Background music
A bowl of water and a towel

Procedure

Before the participants arrive, arrange their chairs in a circle. In the center of the circle, place a table and on the table, a can, a candle, and matches. On the floor, by the table, place a large metal pan. When the group is assembled, light the candle and dim the room lights. Pass out two coins to each person, and ask the participants to hold one in each hand.

Introduce the activity by saying, "This celebration is going to help us gauge the depth of our commitment to follow Jesus. Each of us will decide on an action he or she must take to move along on the journey to God. First, however, let's be quiet and relax for a moment or two." After a pause, say a spontaneous prayer, asking for the Lord's presence during the activity.

Then read aloud the story of the rich young man in Matthew 19:16–22. Help the group reflect on the story by saying, "Following Jesus is not easy. It demands that we allow him to enter the very center of our beings and to touch the very core of our lives. To let Jesus come this close is often so threatening that our defenses immediately go up. Our resistance to this intimacy is like a clenched fist. We want to cling tightly to ourselves, to protect ourselves."

After a moment or two, tell the following story: "An old woman was brought to a medical center. She was wild, snarling at everyone in sight and scaring people so badly that the doctor had to take everything away from her. But she kept her fists so tightly closed that the doctor could not open them. Finally, it took two strong male nurses to pry her fists open. In each one was a small coin. She clung to those coins as though she would lose herself if she lost them. If they were taken from her, she feared she would have nothing more, would be nothing more. Letting go of those two coins was most painful for her. Yet she needed to let go before treatment could begin.

"In some ways, we are like that old woman. We want to hold fast to what is familiar, even though there are things we are not proud of. We delude ourselves by saying, 'I'd like to be different, but not right now.' We find it safer to cling to the past than to trust in the future. We prefer to hang onto a few coins rather than open our hands in surrender to the Lord."

Ask the participants to squeeze their coins tightly in their fists. Then say, "My brothers and sisters, we come before Jesus as did the rich young man, asking, 'Lord, what must we do to follow you?' Jesus tells us that we must let go of whatever is holding us back so that we will be free to follow him. Like the rich young man, we clutch our fists tightly around our coins. Notice how warm the coins have become in your hands, how comfortable they feel, how familiar they are, how precious they are."

Wait a few moments and then say, "Lord, you ask us to give up our last coins in order to follow you. But who wants to do that? We know that we are not perfect. There are things about ourselves we are not proud of, but that's the way we are. We would like to be different, but we can't change right now.

"Brothers and sisters, open your hands. Look at your coins. What are two things that get in the way of your following the Lord? Give the coins names."

When everyone seems ready, read Matthew 16:24–26 and Luke 12:32–34 to the group. Then distribute writing paper and pencils, and have each participant write a letter to Jesus. The participants should briefly describe what the coins stand for in their lives and then ask Jesus for help in letting these obstacles go. If you wish, play some appropriate background music during this time.

After about fifteen minutes, invite the participants to go up to the table one at a time and drop their coins in the can. Explain that this will be a sign that they are willing to let go of those things that keep them from following the Lord. After dropping their coins in the can, they should use the Christ candle to set their letters on fire and then place them in the pan on the floor.

When everyone has finished, take a bowl of water and a towel, and wash the hands of the person on your right. That person should then wash the hands of the next person, and so on, until everyone's hands have been washed. Conclude the activity by asking the participants to join hands and to recite or sing the Lord's Prayer.